STAINED GLASS

STAINED GLASS

Pere Valldepérez

B T Batsford

Stained Glass

Text and projects:
Pere Valldepérez

Lluís Borràs, Pere Valldepérez and Lola
Donaire collaborated in the chapter
"History of Stained Glass".

English translation:
Michael Brunelle
Beatriz Cortabarria

Photography:
Gabriel Serra

Design:
Joseph Guasch

ISBN: 0 7134 8783 6

First published in the UK in 2002 by
B T Batsford
64 Brewery Road
London N7 9NT

A member of **Chrysalis** Books plc

Originally published in Spanish in 1999
under the title *El Vitral* by Parramón
Ediciones, S.A., Barcelona, Spain

© Copyright Parramón Ediciones S. A.

A CIP record for this book is available from the
British Library.

Printed in Spain

Con

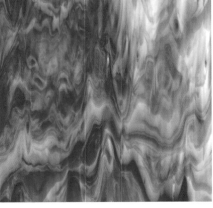

tents

Introduction

This volume is a reference tool in which you can find everything relating to the history, the materials, the tools, and the techniques most commonly used to make stained glass. At the same time, it is a book that will help you get to know and love the art of the stained glass masters, whose works transform the light and the color of interiors, changing them into magical places that satisfy the senses and the spirit.

For these reasons, this volume has been divided into three major parts.

The first part, devoted to the history of stained glass, exlores the main high points of this art, beginning with its origins in the Middle Ages and continuing to the present time, which, thanks to the efforts of the masters, is characterized by intense technical and artistic creativity.

The second part is divided into three sections. The first section gathers all information related to the materials—including the glass, the metal, the lead, and the putty—and to the tools (e.g., for cutting and for assembling). The second section is devoted to the description of the technical aspects, from executing the project to applying patinas. The third section includes several practical projects that demonstrate how to produce different types of stained glass from beginning to end.

The third part gives the reader the opportunity to become familiar with the most common processes of restoration, as well as to get to know step by step two interventions executed by the restorer on respective stained glass projects.

This volume also includes an extensive glossary of definitions of those concepts whose meanings, because of their specific nature, do not appear in average dictionaries.

For those readers who wish to broaden their knowledge of a specific aspect relating to stained glass, an extensive bibliography on the subject is included to serve as a guide.

Even though the term *stained glass* covers an ample array of practices, it is important to differentiate the commercially produced stained glass pieces, such as the ones commonly used as closures for windows and doors, from the artistic stained glass pieces produced by a master artist who is trained to manipulate the glass with an artistic goal in mind, and which is the aspect represented in this volume.

One must always remember that the main working tool of a stained glass master is the hands, capable of transferring an idea, a project, or a dream onto the glass. Furthermore, the author is convinced that creativity and rigidity are not good companions, because to be creative one must transgress the norm, or experiment. However, the technique, the knowledge of the materials, and the use of the appropriate tools are of great importance to be able to execute the designs with mastery and quality. As Leonardo da Vinci said:

Those who fall in love with the practical aspect without the science are like sailors who enter the boat without a rudder or compass and are never certain where they are headed. The practice must always be founded on theory....

Pere Valldepérez, born in Jesús-Tortosa (Tarragona, Spain) in 1946, is a stained glass artist and a restorer of stained glass. He was educated at the Escuela Massana in Barcelona. After winning several national and international prizes, he established his studio in 1975 in the same city in which he studied. He has been a professor at the Escuela Massana since 1989.

Among his many works are a 1,400-square-foot (130-square-meter) assembly of acid-etched glass for the Gaudí room in the Barcelona airport, designed by the architect Óscar Tusquets; three stained glass windows, in the collage technique, designed by the painter Ángel Jové for the University of Lleida; and the 2,100-square-foot (200-square-meter) lamp-skylight for the auditorium in Las Palmas de Gran Canaria, also by Óscar Tusquets. Countries as distant from his birthplace as Zaire and Japan are the recipients of some of his work.

At the same time, his work in the field of restoration has left its impression not only in Barcelona—at places such as Palau de la Música Catalana (Palace of Catalan Music) and Basilica of Santa Maria del Mar—but also in other places in Spain, such as Tarragona, Xativa, and Arucas.

The book *Pere Valldepérez. Vidres, Ilum i color* (*Pere Valldepérez. Stained Glass, Light and Color*), published in 1997, encompasses a large selection of his creative and restoration work.

his chapter presents a brief summary of the history of the process and use of stained glass through the centuries. The use of glass as a translucent closure for windows and other openings was already practiced in ancient times. Glass pieces have been found in Pompeii, Herculaneum, and Rome and in other cities of the Roman Empire.

However, the great development of this art, whose closest ancestors from the technical standpoint are mosaic and enamel, began with the dawn of Christianity and evolved during the Roman and Gothic periods. In the nineteenth and twentieth centuries, after a long period of decline, stained glass emerged strongly and nowadays is one of the most lively and innovative art forms of the artistic world.

In his work the *Diversarum artium schedula*, the monk Theophilus described in great detail the technique for making stained glass, which remained unchanged until the twelfth century, as well as the kilns and the glasshouse pot. Iron shavings and their oxides were applied over the glass to create designs. Once the paste had dried out, the glass piece was covered with lime and was fired in a kiln at a temperature that did not reach the fusion point. The putty, which was applied in the joints between the glass and the lead to prevent rainwater from getting in, was made of ashes and linseed oil.

History of
Stained Glass

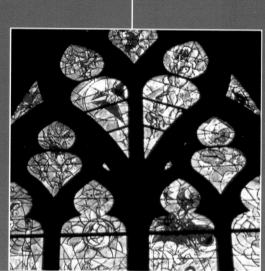

Pre-Romanesque and Romanesque

Pre-Romanesque

The first artistic stained glass pieces preserved date to the Carolingian period. They are not related to architecture but to the sumptuary arts—and more specifically to silver work. The oldest piece found to this day is located in the French cemetery of Séry-lès-Mézieres; it is believed that it was part of a reliquary. It is made of various pieces of glass, all of them joined together with lead, which represent a cross with floral motifs on the sides flanked by the letters alpha and omega.

When the abbey of Lorsch, in Hesse, Germany, was excavated 1932, a very fragmented small stained glass piece depicting the head of Christ was found; it is believed to date back to the latter part of the ninth century or the beginning of the tenth century. The oldest image of Christ preserved intact in a stained glass work of art is another piece depicting the head of Christ from the ninth century that comes from the abbot's church of Wissembourg in Alsace, France.

These remains bear great stylistic similarity, and they can be considered the first samples of western stained glass depicting the human figure. Their study confirms the different techniques described by Theophilus. The way in which the grisaille is applied—with almost grotesque heavy lines, found in the areas of the eyes, hair, and beard—as well as the ochre shading that forms the shadows of the profile have been maintained to the present time.

Romanesque

In the eleventh, twelfth, and part of the thirteenth centuries, the Romanesque style developed in Europe. The large, thick church walls had small openings through which light could enter. In cathedrals and in important churches these openings were protected with stained glass, which was greatly influenced, from the stylistic point of view as well as from the iconography, by miniatures. The most common stained glass works of this time were medallions and depictions of famous people.

In the medallions, biblical scenes, the lives of the saints, and scenes of popular and daily life were represented. The medallions were round, oval, or square in form, surrounded by an iron structure. The borders that followed the perimeter of the medallion served both an ornamental purpose and a practical purpose, which was to adapt the stained glass piece to the size of the opening and to protect the interior glass. (Because the interior glass normally represented scenes, it was therefore more difficult to replace.) In general, these borders were formed by floral or linear motifs of different colors and took up a sixth of the width of the glass.

▲ Stained glass work from the three windows located below the rose window in the west façade of the Chartres Cathedral in France, produced between 1145 and 1155. From left to right, the Passion, the Childhood of Christ, and the Jesse Tree.

In the stained glass panels that represent a single person, the figure is usually monumental in size with very marked features. Such panels were usually placed in the windows of the clerestory.

France was one European country that played an important role in the development of the Romanesque style. In France, the most important stained glass pieces of this style are found in the areas of Le Mans and Poitiers. They all belong to late periods of the Romanesque, and they share the same stylistic influences.

The cathedral in Le Mans houses one of the most important sets of stained glass windows of the period—that is, the scene of the Ascension of Christ, executed in four panels and produced in 1145. The figure of the Virgin presides over the ensemble and is flanked on each side by three apostles. The mastery of the technique and the ease with which the artist was able to combine the colors of the background with the clothing is key.

The stained glass windows of the cathedral in Poitiers, produced in 1162, display great homogeneity and are probably either the work of a single studio or the same school, which planned and executed their work with a unique sense and methodology. Of the entire body of work, the scene of the Crucifixion,

◄ Fragment of the stained glass window from the ninth century, which represents the head of Christ, from the abbot's church of Wissembourg, in Alsace, France. Notice the features profiled with grisaille, which are characteristic of the pre-Romanesque style. Presently, this piece of work is preserved in the museum of Oeuvre Nôtre-Dame of Strasbourg in France.

depicting at the top the Ascension of Christ and at the bottom the Death of Saint Peter, stands out because of its beauty.

However, it is in Saint-Denis and in Chartres where stained glass acquired its own nature when it became integrated into the emerging architecture and architects considered it an element of first order in their buildings. The figure of abbot Suger of Saint-Denis was very important because of the stylistic innovation that it represented, introducing elements that announced the arrival of the Gothic.

The Chartres Cathedral houses three stained glass windows—the Jesse Tree, the Childhood of Christ, and the Passion of Christ—that were produced between 1145 and 1155 and that present a marked influence from those of the abbey of Saint-Denis, the latter of which unfortunately have almost disappeared completely. The ones that survived underwent restoration in the mid-nineteenth century or were spread among various churches and in private collections. The figures of Chartres have left behind the solemnity typical of the Romanesque, and they have acquired movement and expression. In the same cathedral, one can admire the beautiful stained glass window of the Nôtre-Dame de la Belle Verrière (Our Lady of the Beautiful Stained Glass), produced around 1150. This unique work of art has only the four central panels, which depict the Virgin Mary and the Child; the angels around the Virgin Mary were added in the thirteenth century. From a technical perspective, this stained glass window synthesizes all French

knowledge of stained glass windows of the twelfth century, with its incomparable reds and blues and the vitality that the thick contours give them.

The oldest stained glass windows preserved in their entirety can be found in **Germany**: the stained glass windows of the Ausburg Cathedral known as the five prophets because they depict the Old Testament prophets David, Moses, Daniel, Hosea, and Jonah. The figures are more than 6½ feet (2 m.) tall. They were made at the end of the eleventh century in the shop of the Tagernsee Abbey, whose creations are found all over Bavaria.

In **England**, the Cathedral of York houses the oldest stained glass window in England, a piece that corresponds to the representation of the Jesse Tree, or genealogical tree of Christ, and dates to the mid-twelfth century.

The stained glass windows of the twelfth century from the Cathedral of Canterbury were executed with great mastery. The northern rosette, which depicts Moses holding the Ten Commandments, was finished in 1178. The stained glass windows that represent the genealogy of Christ stand out for their beauty and color.

In **Spain**, no remains exist of the stained glass windows of the Romanesque era. However, there are some examples from the Cistercian period. The Cistercian order, which was characterized by the defense of simplicity and austerity of the forms, only allowed geometric adornments on stained glass windows and used virtually no color, with only a touch of red, yellow, and green.

▲ Detail of the Jesse Tree from the Romanesque stained glass windows of the Chartres Cathedral in France, dating back to between 1145 and 1155. Only 1 of the 24 heads that appear in this stained glass window is original to the time period.

◄ Romanesque stained glass windows from the Cathedral of Ausburg in Germany, which represent the prophets Daniel, Hosea, David, and Jonah. In them one can appreciate the solemnity typical of the Romanesque figures and the use of color to define the clothing. They are the oldest stained glass windows in the world that are preserved in their entirety.

Gothic

Gothic architecture had a daring quality that inspired grand and beautiful chapels, churches, and cathedrals. It substituted lighter walls for the thick and heavy Romanesque ones, the groin vault for the barrel vault, and flying buttresses for buttresses. What's more, it allowed for the opening of ample windows and enabled stained glass to acquire a leading role, acting as protection, iconography, and processor of the light that shone through them. At the same time, stained glass emerged as the faithful witness to the stylistic and iconographic evolution of this period, with which its relevance became even greater, and can be compared to that of the other arts, such as painting, miniature art, and sculpture.

The fourteenth century, which from the stylistic point of view comes even closer to the solutions of the Renaissance, was a great advance from a technical point of view, thanks to a series of discoveries that contributed to the evolution of the art of the stained glass makers. One of them, the silver stain, revolutionized the technique. It enabled the artist to paint the glass with different tones of yellow and to eliminate some lead came,

which resulted in larger windows and a richer chromaticity. Another innovation was the use of flashed glass, which is produced by covering a piece of clear or colored glass with another (when it is still in the molten stage), with which more luminosity and color can be achieved. Around 1380, grisaille pointillism was introduced.

France is the country that houses the most important stained glass pieces of the time. The joint body of work from the Chartres Cathedral and Sainte-Chapelle, in Paris, stands out not only for its beauty and technical perfection but also for its representation of two different periods. The influence of these pieces inspired contemporary and later work.

After a fire that occurred in 1194, Chartres began reconstruction of the cathedral. Several stained glass shops were commissioned to produce more than 170 stained glass windows to cover a surface of about 21,000 square feet (2,000 sq. m.). This grand endeavor was possible thanks to the money received from numerous donors who are represented in medallions. Among the impressive body of work, the northern rose window stands out, known as the Rose Window of France, which represents a golden *fleur-de-lis*, and the stained glass of the Zodiac, which narrates the work characteristic for each month of the year, with the exception of January, which is represented by a three-headed man, symbolizing the past, the present, and the future.

Sainte-Chapelle, built between 1243 and 1248 to house the relics of the Passion, was designed as a glass reliquary. The stained glass windows, about 50 feet (15 m.) high, fill almost the entire wall space of the upper chapel. They are framed by pointed arched windows, which display fine tracery work and are completely integrated into the architecture. The skillful use of blues, reds, purples, yellows, and dark green is accentuated by a quick line that gives movement to the figures. The use of grisaille, as if it were watercolor, makes the design less rigid.

The scenes are contained in medallions, and the figures were designed to be in scale with the building. The result is impressive. The

light that passes through the different colored glass transforms the space inside, giving a surreal appearance, almost supernatural.

The stained glass windows of Nôtre-Dame Cathedral in Paris were greatly influenced by those of Sainte-Chapelle. The rose windows of the northern and southern faces were executed with great mastery. The first one, which dates back to the mid-thirteenth century, represents the Virgin Mary in the center, on a throne with Baby Jesus, surrounded by some 80 priests, judges, and kings of the Old Testament. The southern face, finished 10 years later, is dedicated to Christ, accompanied by the apostles, saints, and angels.

In the fourteenth century, the use of grisaille became common practice. The most important shops of stained glass makers were found in Normandy, France. Although the quality of the work did not surpass that of the previous century, interesting stained glass pieces were produced, such as the ones from the Evreux Cathedral and those from the Abbey of Saint-Quen, in Rouen. These pieces show a change of style—that is, a more evolved Gothic style with more movement in the figures, which are more stylized, and with a type of architecture with relief emphasis to frame the space. The frequent use of silver stain is characteristic of this period and this region.

Of the Gothic body of work preserved in **Germany**, the oldest stained glass windows

▲ Rose window from the upper chapel of Sainte-Chapelle, designed to house the relics of the Holy Cross. It is made of more than 1,000 medallions and glass panels.

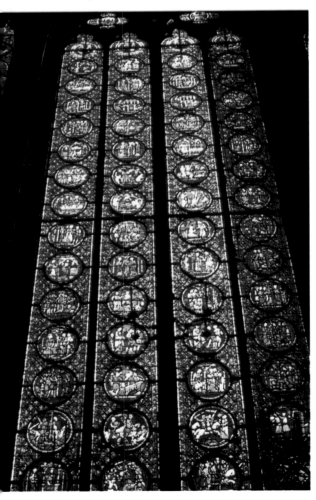

◄ Stained glass windows of Sainte-Chapelle, in Paris, France, depict scenes from the Old Testament and the life of Jesus, Saint John the Baptist, and Saint John the Evangelist.

of the Cathedral of Cologne stand out, dating back to the middle part of the thirteenth century. They measure more than 42 feet (13 m) high and are divided into 11 panels. From the semantic point of view, the scenes from the Old and New Testaments bear a relationship. For example, the scene of Jonah being returned to the beach is a foreshadowing of the Resurrection of Jesus, and that of the Queen of Sheba presenting offerings to Solomon relates to the Epiphany. Also, the Cathedral of Marburg houses some interesting stained glass windows, which represent scenes from the life of Saint Isabel.

The most important German stained glass windows of the fourteenth century are those from the Cathedral of Esslingen; the ones from Heiligkreuztal, of Italian influence; and the ones of Saint John, from the Cathedral of Cologne.

The most important Gothic stained glass windows in England are those from the Cathedral of Canterbury. An analysis shows a clear relationship with the French stained glass. The stained glass window that depicts the martyrdom of Saint Catalina in the church of West Horseley is a clear example of the autochthonous stained glass work. Its figures are more expressive and stylized.

In **Italy**, the stained glass windows of the high Basilica of Saint Francis of Assisi, from the thirteenth century, show a strong German influence, especially pertaining to colors. The scenes that decorate the walls form part of the iconographic cycle of the life of the Virgin Mary and Jesus.

In Italy, the lack of specialized masters in this art promoted the collaboration of an artist painter with the shops that made the pieces. An example is the Cathedral of Sienna, which houses a stained glass window with the scenes of the Death and Coronation of the Virgin Mary, whose drawing is attributed to Duccio.

In the fourteenth century, the painters from Florence and Sienna introduced perspective in stained glass and, with it, volume and proportion. The stained glass windows from the Basilica of Saint Francis, in Assisi, and those from the Santa Croce, in Florence, are clear examples of these technological advances.

In **Spain**, the thirteenth-century stained glass windows from the Cathedral of León must be singled out for their beauty. In the Cathedral of Toledo, the pieces made as early as the fourteenth century, such as the beautiful rose window of the door of the Chapinería, bear a clear French influence. The Italian influence is manifested in the bodies of work of Girona and Tarragona.

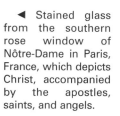

◄ Stained glass from the southern rose window of Nôtre-Dame in Paris, France, which depicts Christ, accompanied by the apostles, saints, and angels.

▼ Stained glass *La Virgen del Dado* (*The Virgin of the Dice*), designed by Nicolás Francés and made by Anequin. An example of international Gothic style, which extended until the middle of the fifteenth century with the work of Nicolás Francés.

▲ Detail of a stained glass window from the presbytery (upper window) of the Cathedral of León in Spain.

The Renaissance

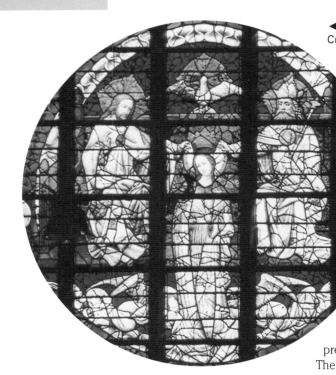

◄ Stained glass window representing the Crowning of the Virgin Mary, preserved in the Church of Saint Gomario, in Lier, Belgium. In this piece, which shows the influence of the Flemish painters, notice the movement of the clothing and the expressions on the faces.

The fifteenth century, the first period of the Renaissance, was a transitional period. While some places were producing art in the Gothic, Flemish, or Italian style, or were adopting forms in the international style, others were experimenting with the new Renaissance formulas, which reached their pinnacle in the next century.

During the fifteenth century, the stained glass windows in the Flemish style became more closely related to painting. In this area, painters such as Van Eyck and Van der Weyden are worth mentioning.

Also, the number of small windows and scenes decreased, replaced by grandiosity and the study of the human figure. Some of the main technical characteristics of stained glass during this period are the heavy lines and the use of a silver stain with filigree backgrounds.

Even though the presence of stained glass windows in churches was questioned in the fifteenth century because of the distraction they caused among churchgoers, during the first part of the sixteenth century they continued to flourish thanks to the religious Gothic architecture. However, in Italy, civil and religious buildings were constructed following new aesthetic guidelines, called the Renaissance style, whose main feature was the revival of the classical past. This transformation of the architectural space affected the concept of the interior, which now appeared diaphanous, in churches as well as in residential and civilian buildings.

Human beings had come to be the center of the universe, and the buildings were erected on that scale. As a result, beginning in the sixteenth century, the work in the stained glass shops decreased; only the Flemish shops maintained their prestige for some period of time. Their masters contributed new ideas, and their presence was requested all over Europe. The Protestant Reform and later the Catholic Reform dealt the final blow to the use of stained glass to decorate churches.

A deep transformation also took place in the technical area. Stained glass windows became a painter's specialty, which reduced the size of the lead caming and increased the size of the glass; the range of colors became lighter, and the color tones obtained in the kiln were accentuated, making the stained glass more luminous. The strong and heavy lines were reduced to profiles, and modeling was done through progressive shading. Perspective was also incorporated, giving compositions more depth.

In **Flanders**, the stained glass windows of the Tournai Cathedral, in Belgium, constitute a good example of the art created in the shops of the master stained glass artists of the fifteenth century; however, their style is still Gothic. In them, historic scenes take the place of religious ones. The stained glass windows of the Church of Saint Gomario, in Lier, reflect the change in mentality, evolving toward themes more typical of the Renaissance than the Gothic. The stained glass window of Charles V of the Brussels cathedral, made in 1537 by Bernard van Orley, is already completely Renaissance.

► Scenery of the Jesse Tree, made by Engrand Le Prince for the Church of Saint-Etienne, in Beauvais, France. Notice the use of the silver stain in the composition.

During the fifteenth century, **France** benefitted from the ideas, forms, and styles that were generated in other parts of Europe. A good example of this is a stained glass window from the Cathedral of Bourges, which shows a clear Flemish influence and whose author applied the technique of flashed glass for the first time.

In France, during the sixteenth century, the Flemish influence gave a new momentum to the stained glass art. Names such as Arnoult de Nimège, who worked mainly in Rouen and adopted Renaissance elements in his compositions, and the Le Prince brothers (Engrand, Jean, Nicholas, and Pierre), whose shop was in Beauvais and who also worked in Rouen, stand out.

In **Germany**, there were notable artists, such as Hans Acker, who produced the stained glass windows of the small chapel of Besserer, of the Cathedral of Ulm, which depict biblical scenes. But most of the stained glass windows of fifteenth-century Germany were created by the master hands of artists who worked in the shop under Hemmel von Andlau, in the city of Strasbourg. Cathedrals from Augsburg, Munich, Tubinga, Salzburg, Friburg, Frankfurt, and Metz housed their creations.

▲ Oculus window at the base of the dome of the cathedral of Florence, Italy, which represents the prayer in the garden. It was made by Lorenzo Ghiberti, a Renaissance painter who depicted a great expressive vitality in this work.

In **England**, stained glass acquired a certain degree of autonomy in relation to what was being done on the Continent. Worth mentioning are the stained glass windows of the collegiate church of Saint Mary of Warwick, the All Souls College in Oxford, and the Cathedral of Canterbury. Important schools were formed, such as the one of Norwick, whose work embellished the walls of many churches, among which the one of Saint Peter Mancroft stands out for its beauty.

From the sixteenth century, a series of stained glass windows from the chapel of King's College in Cambridge stands out because of its vitality and realism and for its perfection in capturing light and shadows.

It is in Florence, **Italy**, where the most innovative creator of the Italian art of the Quatrocento emerged. The influence of the Renaissance painters caused the stained glass masters to employ techniques in their work that belong to painting rather than to stained glass.

The Florentine sculptor Lorenzo Ghiberti designed the three oculus windows of the western façade of the Florence cathedral. The middle one, which represents the Assumption,

▶ The stained glass windows from the sixteenth century preserved in the Church of Fairford, in Gloucestershire, Great Britain, were made, at least in part, by Flemish artists.

stands out for the movement of its angels, who hold the embroidered robes of the Virgin Mary. The two oculus windows that frame it date to a later time; they are dedicated to Saint Stephan and Saint Lawrence. The base of the great dome of Brunelleschi was lighted by eight oculus windows, designed by Ghiberti, Ucello, Castagno, and Donatello. In the same city, Perugino produced the stained glass window of the Coming of the Holy Ghost, and Domenico Ghirlandaio worked on the stained glass windows of the Church of Santa Maria Novella. All these works are examples of artists who came from other arts.

Besides Florence, which during this period enjoyed great artistic splendor, Bologna and Milan should be mentioned. The first because its shops produced stained glass windows of great quality, and the second because its cathedral housed the largest ensemble of stained glass windows in Europe.

In the fifteenth century in **Spain**, the international style coexisted with the Flemish aesthetic introduced through the stained glass masters who came from this European region and settled in the Peninsula.

The stained glass windows of the main chapel of the Cathedral of Seville, which depict the scenes of the Death and Glorification of the Virgin Mary, constitute one of the best examples of the transition from Gothic style to Renaissance style.

The stained glass windows of the Cathedral of León are some of the most important of the Peninsula. Although some were produced in the thirteenth and fourteenth centuries, for the most part they belong to the fifteenth century.

The Cathedral of Barcelona displays on the sides of the ambulatory several stained glass windows produced according to the parameters of the courtly international style. The stained glass window of the baptismal area, which represents the scene of the *Noli me tangere*, is by master Gil Fontanet and is a reproduction of a painting by the Spanish painter Bartolomé Bermejo, from 1495. This stained glass window has some of the elements typical of the Renaissance style, and it stands out for its outstanding use of lines.

The basilica of Santa María del Mar, in Barcelona, also preserves stained glass windows from the fifteenth century. From the set, the great rosette of the western wall stands out, with Flemish tracery and a preponderance of blue tones.

During the sixteenth century, the shops in Spain that were established in the preceding years stayed active, including the ones established in Burgos. During this century, the projects that had started during the previous century were finished, such as the Cathedral of Seville, and new work begun on the cathedrals in Salamanca, Segovia, and Granada.

Seventeenth and Eighteenth Centuries

The seventeenth and eighteenth centuries represented a period of decline for stained glass art. In some regions, like Italy, signs of decline had already appeared in the previous century.

The successive wars and religious conflicts of these centuries contributed to the destruction of stained glass art. For example, the French city of Lorraine, famous for its stained glass, was destroyed in 1640. This contributed to the use of transparent glass, with a new range of enamels.

Also, the new Baroque style was thriving, which required strong light to better show its gilt work, which further undermined stained glass.

When the creative impulse for stained glass art declined, the interest for it also fell, and the windows in existence deteriorated from lack of care. Some were restored with little care, such as the ones from Canterbury, and others were discarded, like the ones in Salisbury and York.

In this era of religious intolerance and armed conflicts, the few stained glass windows that were produced were made for civilian buildings, a phenomenon that began incipiently in the last part of the Middle Ages and that now started to acquire more importance.

The production of stained glass windows in **France** dropped sharply. In the **Flemish** territory, some interesting works were still produced, although the production rate also declined considerably.

In **England**, the university buildings of Oxford and Cambridge received new stained glass windows. Among the artists worth mentioning are the brothers Price, whose shop produced many works. Another renowned English artist was William Peckitt, who made the stained glass windows for the cathedrals of Lincoln and Exeter and the chapel of the New College, in Oxford.

In **Spain**, as in the rest of Europe, many shops were forced to close their doors because of lack of demand. With them, the knowledge acquired during the previous centuries disappeared. Stained glass windows with geometric decorations from the seventeenth and eighteenth centuries are preserved in the Monastery of Pedralbes, in Barcelona; the most famous were produced in 1767 by Josep Ravella. The Basilica of Santa María del Mar, in the same city, also has stained glass windows by this artist.

The Nineteenth Century

The Renaissance of Stained Glass

The historicist spirit of Romanticism, harking back to the Middle Ages, made possible the valorization of stained glass, faithfully resurrecting the formulas of composition of medieval stained glass and disdaining the use of enamels.

Despite the interest in recovering this ancient art from its origins, creativity and originality were lacking; as a result, the ancient models were merely imitated with no new idea contributed. In **France**, the architect Viollet-le-Duc promoted a stained glass restoration program in which imitations were substituted for damaged windows, creating confusion and mixing the concepts of restoration and creation. In **Italy**, the personalistic restoration that the Bertini family carried out on the stained glass windows of the Cathedral of Milan was also very questionable.

▶ Stained glass window that the French architect and painter Eugène Grasset designed in 1884; it is presently preserved in the Musée des Arts Decoratifs, in Paris, France.

◀ Stained glass window that the American artist Louis Comfort Tiffany made in 1893. The use of copper foil as material for support and streaky glass are the characteristic traits of this artist.

In the **United States**, the artists John La Farge and Louis Comfort Tiffany experimented with opalescent glass, which is the antithesis of the main characteristic required of the glass for the medieval stained glass windows.

Also, the pre-Raphaelite painters tried to infuse a new look to stained glass, applying to it naturalistic concepts, supported by the modernistic lyricism.

In **Paris, France**, in 1895, Sigfrid Bing exhibited a series of stained glass panels made with designs or sketches of some of the most important painters of the turn of the century—Vallotton, Bonnard, Vuillard, Toulouse-Lautrec, and others. In the exhibition, he showed a different way of painting outside the canvas, contributing new ideas, colors, and forms to the art of stained glass. At the same time, other artists did not understand or they refused to understand the typical language of the stained glass, halting their technical experimentation.

In **Munich, Germany**, Louis of Bavaria, patron of the arts, founded a state shop that exported glass to the United States, England, and Scotland. This shop also designed 123 passages of the Bible for the Cathedral of Glasgow, in the pre-Raphaelite style; however, the shading has suffered damage as a consequence of inclement weather.

In **England**, the Arts and Crafts movement, which was led by the artist William Morris, promoted the socialization of art, conceiving the craft production of objects for daily use, from furniture to lamps and wallpaper for home use. This revival gave stained glass new momentum. Therefore, famous artists such as Burne-Jones, Rossetti, and even Morris himself devoted themselves to the design of stained glass. The Scottish architect Charles Rennie Mackintosh, one of the biggest exponents of British Modernism, followed these artists and designed beautiful stained glass windows for the tearooms of the Willow, in Glasgow.

In **Spain**, Modernism developed mainly in Catalonia, between the nineteenth and twentieth centuries. The Palau de la Música Catalana, in Barcelona, built by the architect Lluís Domènech i Montaner, is perhaps one of the most complete creations. There, architecture, sculpture, and stained glass are joined together to give way to a work of art of incredible beauty and spectacular nature. Of all the stained glass in the palace, the central skylight of the concert hall stands out.

The architect Antonio Gaudí made an interesting incursion into the world of stained glass by applying a trichromatic technique to stained glass windows for the Cathedral of Palma de Mallorca.

◄ Stained glass of the Christ Church Cathedral, in Oxford, England, with the image of Saint Cecilia. It is one of the many stained glass works that the British painter Burne-Jones designed between 1850 and 1880.

▼ Stained glass windows that decorate the rotunda of the second floor of the house of Lleó i Morera, in Barcelona, made in 1906 in the shop of Rigalt i Granell.

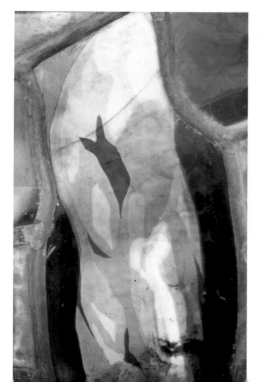

◄ Detail of a stained glass piece that the great Catalan architect Antonio Gaudí designed for the Cathedral of Palma de Mallorca. It shows the trichromatic technique.

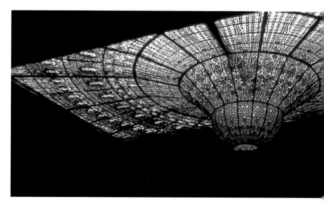

► The lamp-skylight from the main hall of the Palau de la Música Catalana, in Barcelona, is the work of Domènech i Montaner, 1908.

The Twentieth Century. An Open Door to the Future

The reemergence of stained glass art that began in the nineteenth century and that was consolidated by Modernism, causing the number of studios to increase, has continued to develop in the twentieth century, evolving toward very personal forms. The result? More pieces have come out of the shops bearing the hallmark of the artist who made them.

During the twentieth century, stained glass art became universal. The master stained glass makers are now in demand around the world, and their work, experience, and styles are publicized in specialized magazines and books. This is why it is difficult to classify their work by country or style, because the never-ending experimentation with new materials and techniques is their hallmark.

The experimentation with new materials in construction and in the arts in general has given stained glass new momentum, revolutionizing its method of production and allowing an endless array of technical and expressive possibilities that were never expected until now.

During the first 30 years of the twentieth century, the use of iron, steel, and cement in architecture became the norm. The stained glass masters adopted these materials as well, because with them they had increased expressive and technical freedom. Stained glass was introduced in residential and civilian buildings, architecture opened new spaces, and glass factories perfected their industrial methods. In France and in the United States, they began to use dalle to make cement or resin stained glass, merging with the wall of the building. Later, silicone made its debut in the world of stained glass.

In **France**, the great painters of the time participated in the reemergence of stained glass, collaborating in its design. Fernand Léger designed the cement stained glass of the Church of the Sacred Heart, in Audincourt. Marc Chagall worked on the stained glass windows of the Hadassah-Hebrew University Medical Center, in Jerusalem. He designed 12 large stained glass windows dedicated to the tribes of Israel, substituting animals for human figures.

In **Germany**, artists devoted to the design and production of stained glass have shown such creativity through the twentieth century that they have established a typically German style. Anton Wendling designed the great side windows of the choir of the Cathedral of Aquisgrán; they have a geometric design with various intensities of red and blue. Georg Meistermann designed the five-story wall of the radio station in Cologne, Germany, and the huge curved stained glass of the window of the Church of Saint Killian, in Schweinfurt. Ludwig Schaffrath, who used lead to draw lines, also used black and gray in contrast with white, as seen in the stained glass of the train station in Omaya, Japan, which was produced in 1981. Johanes Schreiner, printmaker, painter, and stained glass artist, experimented with architecture in the chapel of the convent of Johannesbund, in Leustesdor/Rhein, substituting stained glass for the walls, giving the convent the appearance of a glass box.

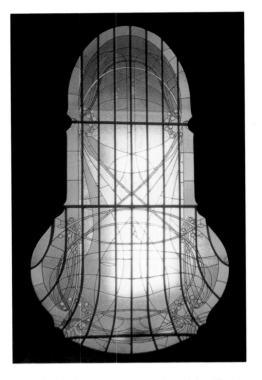

▲ Stained glass piece designed by Hector Guimard for a skylight for the Hotel Mazzara in Paris, France. In this modernistic work, the lead caming forms an active part of the design.

▼ Georg Meistermann produced this stained glass piece in 1958 for the Church of Saint Michael in Solingen, Germany. The liveliness of the flat colors adds an element of surprise to the piece.

◄ The painter Marc Chagall designed this stained glass window for the Cathedral of Saint-Etienne, in Metz, France.

In **England**, the joint work of John Piper and Patrick Reyntiens in the cathedrals of Coventry and Liverpool is worth mentioning. In the former, the symbolic use of colors is surprising, in the latter, the progression of the yellows, reds, and blues displayed in the enormous glass towers.

In **Spain**, some internationally renowned painters have contributed their talents to the world of stained glass. An example worth mentioning is Joan Miró, who designed some stained glass pieces for the royal chapel of Saint Franbourg in Senlis, France; the pieces were produced by the Frenchman Charles Marc. Also, architect Antonio Palacios was the first in the country to use stained glass in cement with industrial glass bricks in the votive temple of the Mar del Paxón, in Nigrán, Pontevedra, in 1935.

In the **United States**, Louis Comfort Tiffany, who lived during the end of the nineteenth century and the beginning of the twentieth, industrialized the technique of stained glass and promoted the decorative arts. He is credited with replacing the lead in stained glass with copper foil. He became famous for his lamps, which were executed with great mastery.

Despite the renewal that this controversial artist introduced, traditional stained glass did not lose ground. A good example of this is the Cathedral of Saint Peter and Saint Paul in Washington, D.C., which recovers the monumental scale characteristic of the Gothic period.

It is the Frenchman Gabriel Loire who gave a new forward push to the production of stained glass in cement in the First Presbyterian Church at Stamford, Connecticut, in 1958. Beginning with this work, hundreds of buildings were built all over the country with windows with glass blocks embedded in the concrete.

Steel was used for the first time for the stained glass windows of KLM, in New York. They are 49 feet (15 m) wide by 16½ feet (5 m) high and were designed by Gyorsy Kepes.

◄ Detail of glass bricks with cement designed by the architect Antonio Palacios in 1935 for the votive temple of Mar de Paxón, in Pontevedra, Spain.

► The American architect Frank Lloyd Wright created the design in 1912 for the Casino in Riverside, Illinois.

▼ Glass ceiling of 23 feet (7 m) in diameter that covers Blakwood Hall in Monash University, near Melbourne, Australia. It was made of fused glass tiles by the Australian artist Leonardo French.

Making
Stained Glass

Materials *and Tools*

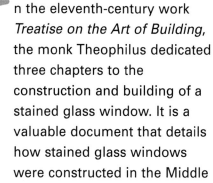

*I*n the eleventh-century work *Treatise on the Art of Building*, the monk Theophilus dedicated three chapters to the construction and building of a stained glass window. It is a valuable document that details how stained glass windows were constructed in the Middle Ages and what materials and tools were used.

Today, the process of glass production has changed, and not only lead is used as support material, but also copper foil, silicone, cement, and so on. Also, with the passage of time, the traditional tools have been transformed and perfected, and new tools have been introduced as a result of the technological development.

Before beginning the process of producing a stained glass panel, it is important to know the function it will fulfill, its location, and the kind of materials that one wishes to use. For example, using blown glass is not the same as using glass made by rolling or glass decorated with texture or held together with lead or silicone.

The material chosen to hold the glass gives name to the type of stained glass window that it is. For example, leaded stained glass is held together with lead; cemented stained glass, with cement; and so on.

The Glass

Production Process

The production of glass dates back to the Bronze Age. It was developed by Greek and Egyptian civilizations. Although each region has used the primary materials in different proportions, the materials that make up the glass are classified in three groups.

Vitrifying Materials

Silica, sand, boric acid, and phosphoric acid. These acid oxides give the glass strength and transparency. Their proportion ranges between 70 and 73 percent.

Melting Materials

Caustic soda and potash. They are basic oxides and the most important ones from the perspective of their use. Their proportion varies between 13 and 15 percent.

Stabilizing Materials

Lime, minium, zinc, aluminum, and barite. They are stabilizing oxides that provide cohesion and resistance. Without them, the glass would fall apart easily from the effects of water vapor and boiling water. The quantity used is from 8 to 13 percent.

To make glass, the materials used must reach a point of fusion—that is, 3,000°F (1,650°C). At this temperature, the pure silica atoms are restructured to form a perfect piece of glass. However, the Romans, because they added lime and caustic soda to the mixture, obtained the glass at a lower temperature. On the other hand, in the Middle Ages, lime and potash were used at a 50/50 proportion, obtaining a faster vitrifying result but lesser quality, because it corroded faster.

Once the gob has been made, sulfur, oxides, and selenium can be added to obtain the color in the paste. For example, blue color may be achieved by using two metals, cobalt and copper; to obtain a neutral blue tone, a small amount of iron oxide can be used, to reinforce the normal dosage of nitrate.

The main coloring products are:
· cadmium sulfur (reddish color)
· antimony oxide (greenish yellow)
· sulphur and coal (black and topaz)
· selenium (red)
· manganese oxide (violet)
· cobalt oxide (blue)
· iron oxide (green, black)
· copper oxide (light blue)

Once the glass ingredients have reached the point of fusion, the glass must be put in a kiln and refired to eliminate and equalize the stresses with a slow cooling process. Once this operation has been finished, the glass is ready for use.

The specific gravity of glass is 2.6. This provides a density of about 162 pounds per cubic foot. Its surface strength—that is, its resistance to scratches—rates 6.5 on the Mohs scale, which is about equal to the hardness of quartz.

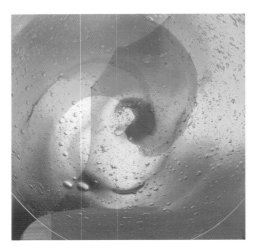

▲ The first glass was spun on a pontil or made by extracting a portion of the glass from the glasshouse pot and placing it on a flat iron surface. This way, the sheet could be cut to the desired size.

▼ Samples of the colors that can be achieved in glass. The colors (more than 400), the textures, and the quality of the glass vary greatly.

▶ **1.** The picture depicts how the glasshouse pot is charged. The silica, the caustic soda, and the aluminum are the components of the charge, which after fusion becomes the glass paste.

▼ **4.** Once the gob has been placed on a flat iron surface, it can be manipulated with tongs to stretch it with a pinch or with scissors to cut it. It can also be blown inside a mold to make containers, it can be placed as a drop to make crown glass, or a cylinder can be made with a blowing iron to obtain glass sheets. For the gob to be manipulated, it must be at a temperature of 1,475°F (800°C).

▲ **2.** After fusion at a temperature of 3,000°F (1,650°C), which has transformed the solid materials into a semiliquid paste, the glasshouse pot is emptied.

◀ **3.** The gob is a very malleable paste, although it has some consistency, which can be manipulated to obtain forms and sheets or blown with a blowing iron. Its extraction from the glasshouse pot can be done using the blowing iron or the pontil (in the picture), which is an iron bar 5 feet (150 cm) long.

▼ **5.** Aided by an oak palette previously moistened with water, the gob placed inside an iron mold is flattened or pressed to make a dalle.

Types of Glass

Nowadays, there are many types of glass. Technology surprises us every day with new additions, especially in the industrial and architectural fields. In this chapter, 11 types of glass most commonly used by stained glass makers have been selected.

Glass

Glass is what we commonly call the gob formed by a mixture of siliceous oxide, potash oxide, and minium or lead oxide. These materials must be of absolute purity in order to obtain the brilliance characteristic of glass pieces.

Strass Glass

Strass glass was produced for the first time in Paris toward the end of the eighteenth century by the artist of the same name. It is basically made of glass rock or white silica, pure potash, a little bit of borax, arsenic acid, potash silicate, and lead silicate and colored with different oxides.

The colored Strass glass pieces are used to imitate sapphire, ruby, and emerald; the noncolored ones, to imitate diamonds. With time, however, strass glass loses some of its brilliance.

▼ Lamp made with Strass glass.

Blown Glass

This method is used exclusively for making stained glass for windows because its characteristics are perfect for this use. It is created the same way it was done in Gothic times, which is why it is also known as antique glass. It is a glass blown in a cylindrical shape; this means that the color variation depends on the thickness of the sheet, which ranges from $1/4$ to $3/4$ inch (2–6 mm). Because this glass does not have a constant thickness, different tones can appear on the same sheet.

▲ The raw material from which glass is produced is quartz (silica). The amount required depends on the grade of purity of the mineral.

Blown glass has two imperfections: the bubbles, caused by the blowing effect and the transfer from the melting place to the working area, and the streaks, caused by a chemical defect (the very components of the glass and the aluminum that can come off the walls of the glasshouse pot) or a physical defect (when a constant temperature has not been maintained). These imperfections, typical of the glass produced in the old days, represent a degree of quality, because the production of this type of glass requires great dedication. Each sheet is unique, and its overall measurements are less than 1 square yard (1 sq. m.). Blown glass is the most sought-after glass by stained glass makers because of its characteristics and great variety of tones.

▼ Blown glass.

Flashed Glass

Flashed glass, whose dimensions never surpass 1 square yard (1 sq. m.), was created to obtain a more luminescent red color. Before, this red color was obtained by adding protoxide of copper and iron shavings to the glass, which produced intense coloration but little transparency when the cylinder came out thick enough to make the stained glass. As a result, the technique of laminated or sandwich glass was invented, which consists of combining a sheet of colorless glass, with enough thickness to make it functional, with a very thin sheet of red glass, to produce the strength, transparency, and luminosity required for use on a window.

One of the procedures used to obtain flashed glass involves submerging the ball of colorless glass, which is at one end of the blowing iron, in the molten red glass in the glasshouse pot, which will then cover the ball. The glass cylinder is created by blowing, and from it the sheet or slab of glass is made.

This technique is currently used to make other glass of various colors. This glass is ideal for treatment with fluoridric acid, which can be applied to the surface to create discoloration, shading, and other effects.

▼ Flashed glass.

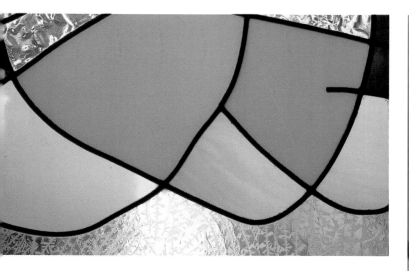

▲ Detail of a stained glass piece made with opal glass.

Opal Glass

The production of opal glass is not the result of a dye extended throughout the gob, but the consequence of the formation of small gas bubbles that form a thick net. These gases are the ones that release the opalescent matter during their decomposition. The bubbles stay in the gob and they reflect the light, which causes the light to be opaque; therefore, the opalescence is caused by saturation. In the old days, opal glass was made using lime phosphate from burned bones; nowadays, it is obtained from fluoride spar. Lime phosphate gives it a marble-like tone. With the fluoride spar, a more milky white is obtained. This type of glass is used as a control over the light, as a diffuser, or as a functional material for making lamps.

▲ Piece made with cathedral glass.

Rolled Glass

Rolled glass is made by pouring the gob over a hot metallic table and working it with the rollers to produce a sheet. This system was already being used in the early days and in the high Middle Ages, but it was rediscovered in 1687. Nowadays, this technique, which is also known as plate glass, is used to produce the large sheets of industrial glass, applying the latest technology.

Cathedral Glass

Cathedral glass is derived from rolled glass. It has a fine texture on one of its sides, which prevents it from being completely transparent; the other side is smooth. This type of glass is used when one wishes to conceal what is behind it.

During the early part of the twentieth century, when stained glass was becoming popular, this type of glass was used all the time because it offered a great range of colors. Its dimensions are usually 8 by 6 feet (250 × 180 cm).

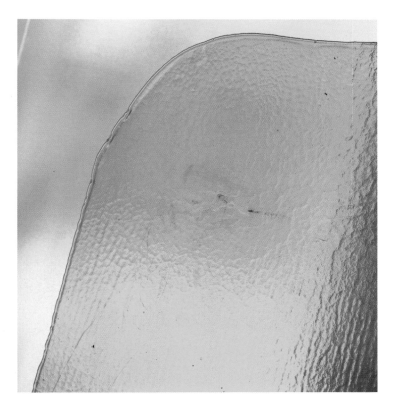

◀ Rolled glass.

Textured Glass

Textured glass is also called pressed glass. It is translucent, and it is made through continuous rolling while the gob is hot. Metallic rollers are used to apply the patterns that give the glass its name. The various forms of pressed glass have heavily patterned textures that create special lighting effects when the light comes through them.

Because these glass sheets are made using industrial processes, they can be of larger dimensions than most of the previous types of glass, about 8 by 6 feet (250 × 180 cm).

▼ Textured glass.

▼ Dalle.

Tiffany Glass

Created by Louis Comfort Tiffany, Tiffany glass is known as American glass in Europe. It is a type of glass produced using a molding process whose colors create a water-like effect, usually in combination with a white from the opalescent family. The mixture of various oxides gives the glass different colors on the surface. It is a type of glass called interpretative because, depending on the direction of the cut, it can resemble a tree trunk, the clouds in the sky, the feathers of a bird, and so on. Its opalescence makes this glass appropriate for use in lighting fixtures.

Rondels and Glass Jewels

The name *rondel* refers to a glass piece made with a mold. A gob of the desired color is placed in a mold to form shapes that intensify the tone of the color. The most commonly known pieces, because of their antiquity, are the rondels, but there is a countless array of samples and shapes.

Dalle

A dalle is a type of glass of about $^3/_4$ inch (20 mm) thick and about 8 by 12 inches (20 × 30 cm) in size. It is produced in the same way as a rondel, being taken out of the glasshouse pot with a solid iron bar about 5 feet ($1^1/_2$ m) long; this bar is called the pontil. The dalle is then deposited in a mold and flattened with a wetted wooden board to achieve the dimensions indicated above. The paste need not be pure. It comes in a variety of colors and to make the light sparkle on the glass, facets can be cut by chipping the edges of the glass when shaping the piece. It can be cut using a glass cutter, a hammer, and a scoring tool or using a diamond disc cooled with water.

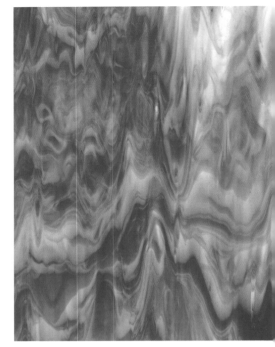

▲ Tiffany glass or American glass.

▼ Rondels and glass jewels.

▶ The photo shows a figure made with grisaille. Notice the outlines and shading effects used to create an exact replica of a piece of sculpture.

Grisaille

Grisaille is a vitrifiable paint that is generally black or brown in color. It is made of iron or copper oxide with borax as a solvent. After a firing process at a temperature of about 1,130°F (610°C), the grisaille becomes bonded to the glass. In order to be used as a paint, it may be diluted with vinegar, water, or turpentine, or as it was done in the old days, with mineral spirits and animal bile. For the paint to adhere to the glass it is necessary to add a few drops of gum arabic, which gives it the consistency required to work with it before firing in the kiln.

This is the main product that the stained glass artist uses for painting on the glass. It is always applied on the inside of the stained glass, but sometimes it is used for touching up the exterior side to reinforce the shading. Depending on how diluted the paint is, the artist can control the amount of light that can go through. When the paint is applied in thick lines, it is called outline or *trait*. If it is used softly, as if it were a wash, it is called *lavis*.

In the fifteenth century, quite by accident, silver stain was discovered, which consists of silver and ochre, and it is adhered to the glass through firing, without the use of a solvent. With this, one can apply color to the outside face of the glass. In the fifteenth and sixteenth centuries, this color was commonly used for the hair, clothing, and so on. This discovery gave way to the creation of colored grisaille like the yellow, green, blue, and others.

Sanguine is another grisaille that is also known as Jean Cousin. It is a fusible paint of a reddish earth tone, which was used in the fifteenth and sixteenth centuries to represent the flesh and which was applied on the outside of the glass. Now it is very difficult to find.

Enamels

Enamel colors are very lively, but are less luminous than grisaille colors. They were used to give the stained glass of the classic, neo-Gothic, and Modernist periods a touch of sophistication.

This fusible paint has colorless enamel as a base, which is formed with glass that melts quickly and easily, so the oxides that provide the color do not vaporize. Their melting point should never surpass 1,112°F (600°C). Below is a list of the products that provide the color:

· cobalt oxide (blue)
· chromium oxide, pure copper dioxide (green)
· antimony oxide, ammonium salts, alum, and gypsum (yellow)
· copper oxide (red)
· iron oxide, manganese peroxide, and, if a darker shade is desired, a little cobalt (black).
· ferric oxide and tin oxide (orange).

▶ Piece painted with enamels. Notice how the colors do not have the same intensity and body as the grisaille. Enamel is more transparent.

Structural materials

For centuries, lead was the only material used to support stained glass. However, the technological advances and experimentation carried out in the field of architecture throughout the twentieth century have introduced new materials, whose properties apport increased lightness to stained glass and have allowed, from an artistic point of view, the development of designs that are more daring and avant-garde.

Lead

Galena has been the most common mineral from which lead has been extracted—which always contains greater or lesser amounts of other metals, such as silver, iron, zinc, copper, and bismuth. Lead is a heavy metal; its specific weight is 25 pounds (11.34 kg) at 61°F (16°C). It is bluish white, shiny, soft, and very malleable. When contact with the air produces oxidation, lead acquires its characteristic grayish color. Because of these qualities, it was the metal of choice during the Middle Ages for joining the various pieces of glass that formed the stained glass piece. However, the lead not only serves as a support, but it also forms part of the drawing and design of the stained glass piece.

The lead came (the cast lead rods that hold together panes of glass) comes from the foundry in rolls weighing 55 pounds (25 kg), with H shaped channels. These rolls are put

through the lead stretcher, after which they can be cut and shaped as desired.

Lead came has two parts: The heart is the inside part that gives the came rigidity; it bears markings, or teeth, to better support the glass and the glazing compound. The faces are the parts whose rounding action keeps the glass in place. The surface of the face is the point of reference when identifying the size of the came; so, for example, if the came is $3/16$ inch (5 mm), then the surface of the face has this dimension. In the twelfth and thirteenth centuries, the heart was very thick and strong and the faces rounded and narrow. The faces, depending on their shape, can also be called flat faces, round faces, and so on. It was not until the fourteenth century that the lead stretcher was used to flatten the lead.

Copper Foil

Copper foil was the first structural material that broke with the traditional techniques. Its main difference with respect to the lead is that it is a much lighter material. Tiffany used it frequently, especially for lamps that were used for residential decoration.

Consisting of a small copper strip with an adhesive side, copper foil is wrapped around the perimeter of the glass piece. It is available in different widths, according to the thickness of the glass used. For example, the strips of $3/16$ or $1/4$ inch (5 or 6 mm) are appropriate for glass that is $3/32$ or $1/8$ inch (2.5 or 3 mm) thick. To assemble the work, the glass pieces wrapped with the foil are placed over the drawing and joined with solder, creating a connection that is strong and versatile.

◄ Different shapes of lead came. The ones most commonly used are $3/16$, $1/4$, and $3/8$ inch (5, 7, and 10 mm).

Concrete

Reinforced concrete as support material for stained glass came into use during the first half of the twentieth century. It is usually reserved for supporting dalle.

To make the reinforced concrete, sand or marble dust is mixed with white or gray Portland cement in a proportion of 10 to 3 or 4 by weight. This is mixed with water to make a mortar, which is poured over a grid of steel rods with a $1/8$-inch (4-mm) diameter.

This material produces solid panels that are comparable to walls. From the artistic point of view, the concrete transforms the fine lines of the lead into expressive lines, giving the stained glass a distinctive character.

▲ Notice the partition of the walls in this stained glass work made with concrete.

▼ Copper foil.

▲ Lead before being stretched.

Silicone

Silicone, which contains silex, an ingredient that is also found in glass, perfectly adheres to the various parts in a stained glass piece. This material, like many others used these days, is the result of the research carried out in the United States in the 1930s to create heat-resistant insulating materials for electrical components.

Silicone is a liquid or pasty material that turns into an elastic solid with excellent mechanical properties when it comes in contact with the humidity in the air because of a curing agent in the formula. It begins to set 3 hours after exposure to the environment, and dries completely in 5 days. It maintains its consistency and will not run, and its properties will not change over time. Any type of glass can be bonded with self-leveling silicone.

▲ Guns for applying the silicone.

Putty, or Mastic

Putty, or mastic, is a paste made with linseed oil and calcium sulfate (gypsum). The linseed oil is extracted from the seeds of the mastic tree, a perennial bush of resinous aroma and purple flowers and fruit that grows in drupes in the Mediterranean forests. The amount of calcium sulfate that is added to the oil varies according to the desired consistency of the putty. The premixed product is available for sale in specialized stores.

The putty holds the glass and the lead in place, preventing rainwater from entering through the joints of the glass. Therefore, it is important to apply it carefully and to check it to make sure it has penetrated the joints. Turpentine or any solvent may help thin the putty and maximize penetration.

▲▼ The only silicone types appropriate for use in stained glass are the ones known as monocomponents R-35 and R-36, which have been experimented with in the laboratories of the French company Rhône-Poulen. The self-leveling silicone R-36 is very liquid and very transparent. The R-35 type is also transparent, but it has a consistency similar to the commonly used silicones. They are both acidic and have a vinegar-like odor.

▼ Clockwise: universal solvent, for thinning putty to aide in penetrating into the sides of the lead; linseed oil (in the cup) to better bind the putty; gray color putty; flat brush to apply the putty inside the lead; black organic dye (in the dish) to dye the yellow putty and to give it a gray tone; yellow putty.

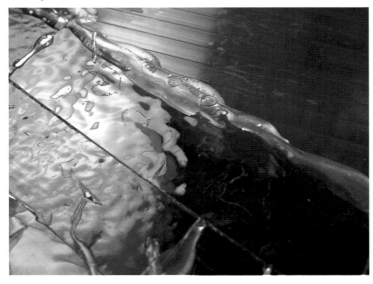

The tools of the stained glass artist are similar to those of the glazier, although more specialized. Their form and use have not changed too much over time. In fact, new tools have been added as the concept of stained glass has evolved and has incorporated other materials.

The majority of the tools that the stained glass artist uses are for personal use and never shared, because with time their shape changes according to the pressure applied with the hand.

In the past, stained glass artists made their own tools, adapting them to their needs. However, nowadays, specialized stores sell tools that are of great quality and that have been designed for an increasingly demanding public.

The Shop

If tools are necessary for making a stained glass piece, so too are the space and the furniture. The shop of a stained glass artist should fulfill two requirements: It must be large, to be able to handle and store the glass comfortably, and it must have natural light, needed to choose the appropriate glass to make the stained glass piece. Also, when it gets dark and artificial light is needed, that light should have the same tone and intensity as the natural light. There are special lamps that reproduce natural light quite closely.

Equipment

Light Table

The light table must have a frosted glass to diffuse the glare from the lights. The table can be either horizontal or vertical. On it, the artist can paint, clean, and study the stained glass piece when carrying out a restoration.

▶ Interior of a stained glass artist's studio.

▼ Light table.

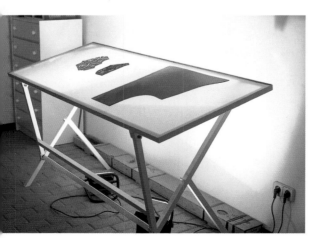

Storage for the Glass

The first piece of equipment that the artist must keep in mind when putting together a shop is shelving for storing and organizing the glass. The equipment must be made of wood, with compartments for glass pieces and sheets of different sizes. The compartments do not have to be very large, only about 12 to 16 inches (30–40 cm), where the glass is classified by color, characteristics, and so on. The compartments should not be overfilled so it will be easier to remove and handle the glass.

A storage shelf is a common piece of equipment for both the glazier and the stained glass artist.

Cutting Table

Another piece of equipment that is common to the stained glass artist and the glazier is the cutting table, which must be large. It is also used for making full-size drawings. It should be kept very level.

Assembly Table

The assembly table is specific to the shop of the stained glass artist. The dimensions can vary, according to the needs; the most common ones measure 80 by 48 inches (200 × 120 cm), and they are 34 to 40 inches (95–100 cm) high. The table must be made of good quality wood and have a rigid and resistant surface. When the surface becomes worn, it must be replaced with another one. It is used for all assemblies, and nails are driven into it to hold the glass pieces. The holes left on the surface by the nails are usually filled in when putty is applied to the stained glass. For the most part, the assembly is done while standing. If one wishes to carry out the assembly sitting down, the height of the table stays the same and a high stool is used for the task. Keep in mind that depending on the tasks, working from the sides of the table may be required; therefore access must be easy and comfortable.

▲ Shelving for glass.

▼ Assembly table.

▼ Cutting table.

Tools

Because there is a large variety of tools, they have been classified in three groups: cutting tools, abrasive tools and brushes, and assembling tools.

Cutting Tools

Glass can be made into any desired shape using cutting tools. Normally, each stained glass artist has his or her own cutting tools, because they adapt to the pressure applied to them. The most important are:

Steel Glass Cutter

This cutter is the most economical. It has a wood handle with teeth to break or groze the glass. It has six wheels of especially tempered thin alloy steel, of which only one is used. When this one wears out, the head is rotated and the work continues with one of the other wheels. To make the wheels last longer, they should be lubricated with mineral oil. Each tip has a felt ring, like a cushion, that serves as a well for the oil that lubricates the wheel and its axle.

Carbon Steel Glass Cutter

This type of cutter has a single tip that can be changed. The handle is short and fitted to the hand. It is easy to handle and allows the artist to see the line where the cut is to be made.

Tungsten Carbide Glass Cutter

This has a mineral oil well in the handle, which helps to keep the wheel in good shape. The tip of this cutter is smaller than the previous one, and when it wears out, the entire head must be changed.

Pistol Grip Cutter

This cutter has been designed to cut glass with a thickness of $^3/_8$ to $^3/_4$ inch (10–19 mm). Its handle has a comfortable grip, and it is held as if it were a hammer. The handle houses the lubricating well.

Diamond Glass Cutter

This had been the most efficient cutting tool until the appearance of the cutters mentioned above. But even now, the artist who owns this tool and knows how to use it can cut any type of glass, especially the hardest ones.

Grozing Iron

Although this tool is not used for cutting, it is necessary for finishing certain types of cuts. It has an iron or brass tip with a series of notches of various thicknesses and rectangular shapes, and sharp edges that are used to groze the glass and to remove jagged points. It can be inserted in hard-to-reach places. The ball at the end is used for separating the scored glass with a blunt blow.

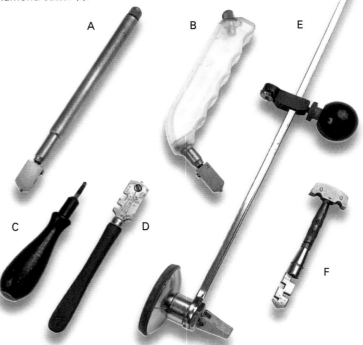

▼ Tungsten carbide glass cutter (a), pistol grip glass cutter (b), carbon steel glass cutter (c), steel glass cutter (d), circle cutter (e), diamond cutter (f).

Circle Cutter

This is used to cut circular shapes of a considerable size. It has a suction cup that adheres to the glass, and it can be adjusted by moving the cutter along the arm.

Lens Cutter

This machine is similar to the previous one, but it works a little differently and cuts smaller circles. It rests on a vertical axis, and it is turned with a handle.

Disc Cutter

This machine has a diamond disc that is kept cool with water, preventing the disc and the glass piece from getting hot. It can be used to cut glass of a considerable thickness, such as $^3/_4$ inch (20 mm).

Optician's Cutter

This small machine is appropriate for cutting small glass pieces. The base cylinder travels with the glass and the wheel presses onto the surface, scoring the glass as any other wheel would.

◄ Lens cutter.

► Disc cutter.

▲ Optician's cutter.

▼ Cutting box with all the tools needed for its use.

▲ Glass cutting pliers (a), running pliers (b), breaking pliers (c), grozing pliers (d), common pliers (e,) grozing iron (f).

Cutting Box

This primitive device is used to cut sheets of marble and glass. With a blunt blow applied above the score made by the cutter, the cutting box functions as a wedge and snaps the sheet of glass in two. It is only used for cutting dalle.

Glass Pliers

Nowadays pliers of many different kinds are commercially available.

Running pliers used to snap scored glass are made of aluminum. The rounded clamps can always be adjusted to 90 degrees with respect to the scored line; the length of the cut is controlled by applying pressure on the pincers.

Various types of pliers are available for grozing or roughing, from wide jaw pliers to needle-nose pliers. They are all made of a soft iron that allows the artist to grind the glass without breaking it.

The breaking pliers have jaws that are 1 inch (25 mm) wide. They hold tightly to the glass surface, and they are used to snap it apart.

Common pliers have many uses. They are used for pulling out nails, for cutting wire, and even for grozing the glass.

Cutting pliers are used to cut glass of up to 1/4 inch (6 mm) thick; they have a hard metal tip.

Pattern Shears

Also known as pattern scissors, these shears have three blades that make a double cut. One of the blades is the same width as the thickness of the heart of the lead came, so they can cut out a strip of about $1/16$ inch (1.75 mm). There are also specific scissors for cutting copper foil; in this case, they leave a space of $1/32$ inch (1 mm). The designs of patterns for leaded or copper foil stained glass pieces are cut out with these scissors.

Common Scissors

Common scissors are used to cut around the outsides of the patterns for the leaded stained glass and to cut the patterns for cement and silicone stained glass work. They are also used for cutting the faces of the came when a piece is needed for repair.

Utility Knife

This knife is very useful for cutting the paper and the board used for full-size drawings.

▼ Pattern shears (a), common scissors (b), utility knife (c).

▲ Silicone carbide block and diamond sanding paper.

▲ Electric grinder.

▼ Abrasive disc.

Abrasive Tools and Brushes

Handling glass carries a high level of risk. That is why it is important to be as careful as possible and to try to minimize the risk of accidents by using the tools properly and by polishing the edges of the cut pieces when necessary.

Silicone Carbide Block

This is used to polish the edges of the glass. It is a good idea to wet it before use to prevent the glass dust from spreading.

Diamond Sanding Paper

This has an abrasive diamond surface, and its special configuration reduces the work significantly and makes it long-lasting. It is advisable to wet the paper to prevent the glass dust from spreading.

Electric Grinder

This water-cooled machine, with a diamond bit, is very useful for polishing the edges of glass. It is also used to cut shapes. Once the polishing is finished, copper foil is very easily applied.

Abrasive Disk

This consists of many silicone carbide flaps. There are different grits available, like 80 grit, which removes glass easily, or 200 grit, which will apply a lighter polish. Water is not required. It will easily attach to any size portable drill.

Belt Polisher

This machine is only found in the shops of professional stained glass artists. It is used to smooth the edges of glass pieces with a continuous abrasive band that is cooled with water. With a finer belt, it can also be used to polish the edges of the glass.

Brushes

Brushes are useful and necessary tools in the stained glass artist's shop. They can be of different types, including both vegetable fiber and wire brushes.

Esparto brushes are used to clean the glass after glazing compound has been applied and are also used for general cleaning. They are available in different sizes and can be made of plastic.

Esparto brushes made with finer vegetable fibers are also helpful. They are used to clean the finishes of the stained glass and to clean the worktables. To create a satin patina a worn vegetable fiber brush should be used, to vigorously buff the lead came and the solder joints.

Wire brushes can be made of steel, bronze, or brass. They are used to scrape off the old lead so new tin solder can be applied. They can also be used to dry clean the surface of the glass—carefully, so the glass is not scratched.

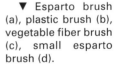

▲ Belt polisher.

▼ Esparto brush (a), plastic brush (b), vegetable fiber brush (c), small esparto brush (d).

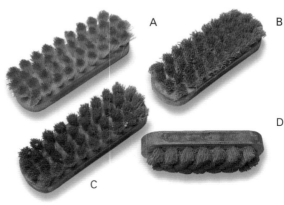

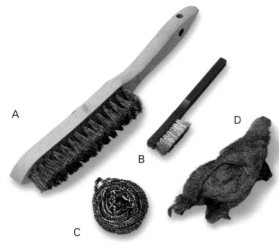

▶ Brushes for outlining *trenars*, for dappling, interlocking, filleting, smear shading, and so on (a), outlining brushes with more bristles to make thicker lines, like the ones known as *trait* (b), small brushes for touching up lines or details (c).

A

B   C

▲ Brush with steel bristles (a), brush with brass bristles (b), stainless steel scrubbing pad (c), aluminum scrubbing pad (d).

Metal Scrubbing Pads

These are used for the same applications as the metal brushes, but they can be made of aluminum or stainless steel. They are useful for cleaning any surface that is hard to reach. They do not leave scratches.

Paintbrushes

These are available in many types and qualities. They can be chosen according to the particular need.

Outlining brushes can be found in various sizes, but they must all have long bristles. Those used for filleting (*trenars*) are made from the hair of an ox's ear. They can be shaped as needles, swords, and so on. They are used for diapering, interlocking, outlining, smear shading, and *trait*. They can also be used to draw with asphaltum and to work on projects involving acid.

The paintbrushes have many bristles. They are used to transfer the grisaille or the enamels from the palette to the glass surface. They can also be used to make strong lines. The bristles are made of thin hair from a marten or a badger.

The badger blender is a wide flat brush, and it is made of authentic badger hair. The bristles are about 4 inches (10 cm) long. This brush is used to diffuse or blend the lines made with other brushes and to apply a wash or *lavis*, and to do stippling. It comes in various widths.

The modeling brushes must be used when the paint is dry but before the glass is inserted into the kiln. They give personality to the work of art, because each brush is different and the artist chooses one based on preference and comfort. They can have short and round bristles, soft or hard bristles, fine, thick, and so on. They are used for stippling, creating minute points of light over the surface of the paint. Using them dry, a highlight or *enlevé* effect is achieved.

Machine for Stretching Lead Came

This machine is used to give the desired gauge to the lead strip. It consists of several bearings that thin the strip by means of rollers that are $3/16$ inch (5 mm) thick, with teeth placed $1/16$ inch (2 mm) apart that pull the strip. Once the strip has been sized, the final bearings with the finishing rollers are installed, to give it a smoother finish. The bearings shape the faces of the lead came, and the rollers create the heart.

There are bearings that produce different sizes and shapes. Nowadays, ready-to-use lead came can be found in stores that sell tools for stained glass making.

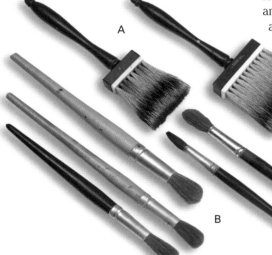

▲ Two types of badger blenders (a), different types of paintbrushes (b).

◀ Modeling brushes.

▶ Machine for stretching lead came.

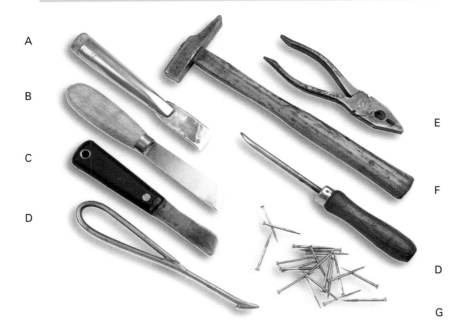

▲ Leading knife with a handle to pound nails (a), leading knife with a wooden handle (b), spatula (c), lathekins (d), pliers (e), hammer (f), glazing nails (g).

▼ 100-watt soldering iron with a flat tip (a), 100-watt soldering iron with a chisel tip (b), 75-watt soldering iron with a flat tip (c), thermal soldering iron (d), pointed tip soldering iron (e).

Tools for Working with Lead

Many tools are used for working with the lead caming. Listed below are the most commonly used. First, however, it is important to note that glazing nails must be used. They should be made of tempered and polished steel and should be 1½ inches (36 mm) long, with a conical, sharp end to make it easier to insert the nails.

Hammer

This tool is indispensable in any shop. There are different types of hammers, including rubber, ball peen, and pointed. Leading requires a light hammer with a steel head for striking the nails and a wood handle, preferably beech, for tapping the corners of the glass and adjusting them to the lead came.

Leading Knife

This is a steel tool with a wood handle that is used for cutting the lead came. It is a good idea to keep it very sharp at all times; otherwise, it would crush the lead came instead of cutting it. It can be sharpened using a steel spatula.

Lathekin

This consists of an iron or wooden rod that ends in a point and has a wood handle. It is inserted between the face and the heart of the lead came with the purpose of opening it and straightening it. It is ³/₁₆ inch (5 mm) wide.

Spatula

The spatula is used to apply putty and to round off the lead came by pressing it against the heart of the came. Because a wooden spatula does not cut, it cannot damage the lead came or the glass.

Soldering Tools and Materials

Soldering is required to connect the web of lead or copper foil that holds the glass together. The tools and products used for this task are described below.

Soldering Iron

This iron is an electric tool (100 watts) that is shaped like a hammer. It has a copper tip ⁵/₈ inch (16 mm) in diameter ending in the form of a chisel. It is ideal for soldering reinforcing bars or angles.

Thermal Soldering Iron

This iron consists of two arms; one of the ends is rounded and is used to solder edges, and the other has a chisel shape for soldering angles. It has an operating temperature is of 572°F (300°C). A thermostat incorporated in the unit prevents the iron from surpassing the desired temperature. It is very useful for restoration projects.

75-Watt Soldering Iron

This iron is ideal for soldering small lead came. Its working temperature is lower than the thermal soldering iron; therefore, it can be better controlled when soldering with tin.

Pointed Soldering Iron

This iron has a small point for use in hard-to-reach places. It holds a small amount of solder and makes small joints.

Tin

Tin is a white and shiny metal whose main properties are its ductility and malleability. It oxidizes when melted, turning into tin oxide when cooled. Mixed with lead it can be used to solder metals. It is sold in strips that contain 60 percent tin and 40 percenrt lead. This solder has a silvery color. If a grayer tone is desired, the proportion must be of 33 percent tin and 67 percent lead.

Flux

Flux is a paste that is available in solid form and contains inorganic acids, such as nitric, sulfuric, and phosphoric acids. The latter causes this product to be a good tin conductor when soldering. Some artists make their own flux from stearin. In order to make a paste that works well, the stearin must be mixed with rosin and olive oil.

▼ Solder bars (a), rosin (b), stearin (c), olive oil (d).

Types of Kilns

In the old days, pieces of glass were fired one on top of the other, separated by a thin layer of gypsum that served as insulation. For this reason restorers sometimes find streaks made by the silver stain that seeped through one of those insulating layers during the firing process. Obviously, today's electric kilns simplify the firing process and are much safer.

Front-Loading Kiln

This is the traditional electric kiln, with heating elements in all four side walls and at the bottom, made with platinum-radium (pyrometer) and either an automatic or a manual temperature regulator. This kiln will last a long time, and it can reach a temperature of 2,400°F (1,300°C) because it is also used to fire ceramics. The firing temperatures that the stained glass artist requires range between 1,022° and 1,150°F (550–620°C).

Firing is done in layers. The painted pieces of glass are placed on top of a steel sheet, which has previously been layered with dehydrated gypsum. The different sheets of steel are separated from each other with steel or ceramic spacers. The dehydrated gypsum powder, which can be purchased in specialized stores, only requires a single previous firing, placing the powder on the trays and letting the temperature rise to 480°F (250°C). When it is taken out, the surface of the powder will have cracked. If the glass pieces had been in the kiln, the cracks would have been imprinted on them, ruining the design. It takes 3 to 5 hours for the temperature to reach 1,150°F (620°C), depending on the load being fired; then the pieces must cool for 48 hours before they are taken out. This kiln cools down slowly, compared to the more modern ones, because its walls are made with refracting bricks, and the outside is made of steel sheet with an insulating material between the two walls. This causes the cooling process to be quite slow.

When purchasing this type of kiln, it is important to keep in mind its power requirements to be sure that sufficient electric power is available; however, many of these kilns can be operated using household power and do not consume a great amount of electricity.

◀ Front-loading kiln.

Top-Loading Kiln

Also called a single-level kiln, this kiln provides a greater firing and cooling speed than a front-loading kiln. The interior walls are layered with a high-density ceramic fiber. The exterior walls are lined with steel. Its heating elements are covered with protective quartz. A microprocessor allows for temperature control through a pyrometer, which is very accurate in temperature and firing time, and it has a programmed automatic turn off. It should be placed in a draft-free area. Grisaille can be fired in 12 minutes and be removed in 30 minutes from this kiln. It consumes a minimal amount of power, and larger pieces can be fired in it than in the traditional kilns. These kilns are designed to be used for thermal forming and fusion and can reach temperatures of up to 3,500°F (1,900°C).

Based on observation and experience, the temperature can be interpreted from the color of the fire. This color is only visible in an oxidizing environment, such as during the firing of grisaille or ceramic enamels. Therefore, although at about 932°F (500°C) no color is noticeable, between 1,022° and 1,112°F (550–600°C) the inside of the kiln acquires a reddish color, similar to the sky when the sun sets. Between 1,112° and 1,292°F (600–700°C) it begins to darken, turning a darker red at 1,454°F (790°C), and to cherry red, orange, light yellow, bright white, and bluish color at 2,732°F (1,500°C).

▶ Top-loading kiln.

Technical *Aspects*

In any artistic discipline, the mastery of the technique is essential. Technique gives the artist the tools required to carry out any artistic project, opening the doors to endless creative possibilities. The knowledge even allows the artist to "break the rules." Thanks to the technique and to its evolution through the centuries, stained glass continues to enjoy great vitality and development to this day. There are many people around the world who devote themselves to experimenting with new techniques and materials, and their creations are more and more innovative and beautiful.

Consequently, the following pages are devoted to an explanation of the techniques used to make stained glass from beginning to end. Besides knowing the materials and the tools needed to create a stained glass project, the artist must also know how and when to use them, how to cut the glass so it does not break, how to apply lead caming to the glass edges, how to connect one piece of lead came to another, what the order of the procedures is to achieve the best final result, and so on.

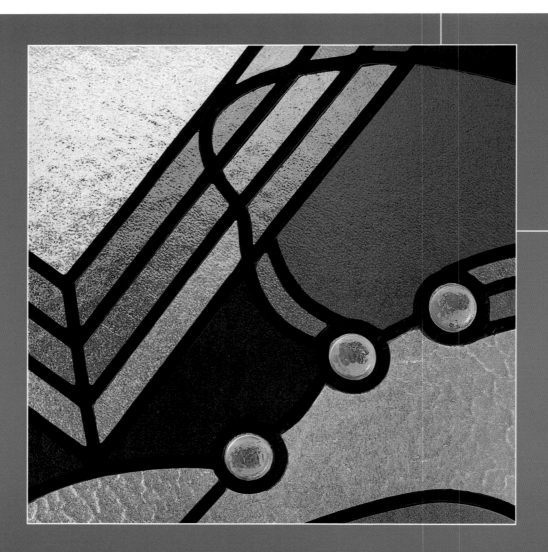

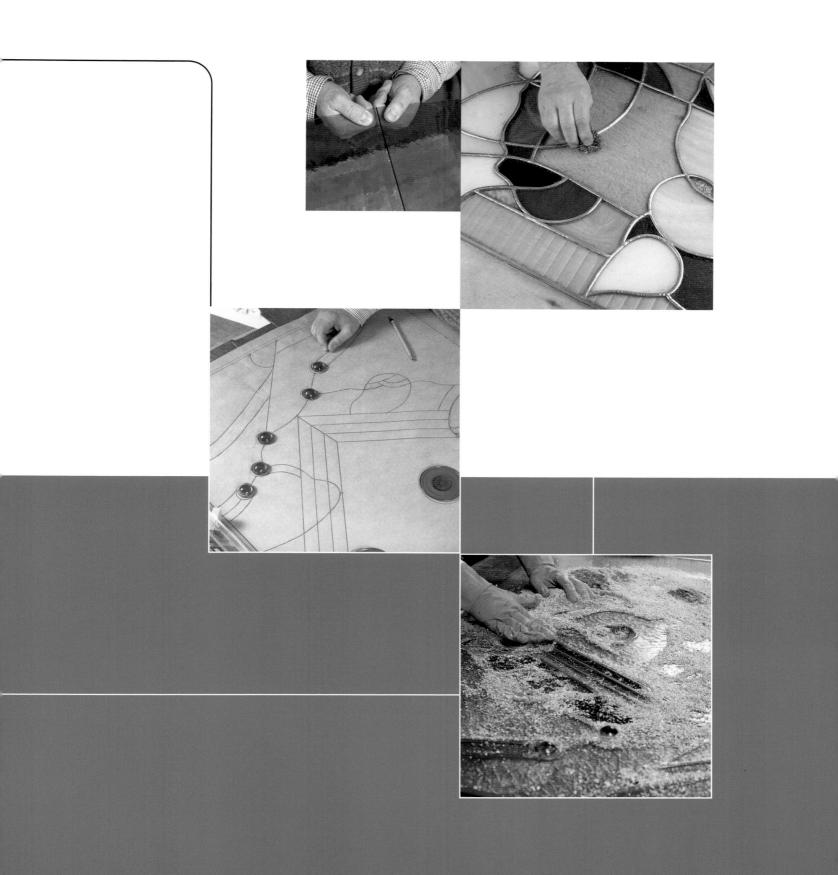

Designing the Project

In the old days, stained glass windows were designed and made inside the very building where they were going to be installed, to dress and embellish its walls. Nowadays, stained glass is made in the studio and is later transferred to its final location. So, before a sketch is done, observe and analyze the space where the stained glass will be installed, and consider the amount and quality of natural light that will come through it.

The **sketch** is the first step that the artist takes to define an idea—that is, to give shape to it. In the production of stained glass, the sketch constitutes the design stage; it is not a quick sketch but an elaborate drawing.

In the **design** stage, the previously sketched idea is finalized and is given a definite form. To carry out the stained glass project, it is necessary to have information about the color of the glass, the quality, the construction with the lead came lines, the assembly, and the structure where the piece will be placed. Also, the dimensions of the stained glass piece should be drawn to scale.

A **prototype**, or mock-up, is made if the design drawing does not have enough information. The model built to scale takes the artist closer to the real work. All the possible problems that could arise during the production process—be it the color, the dimensions, the volume, or the proportions—should be resolved in the prototype phase, because once the project begins, it is very difficult to make modifications, unless the changes are very minor.

A scale of 1 inch to the foot is commonly used, and if the project is very large, 1/2-inch to the foot or smaller can be used.

▲ To make the first drawing or sketch, a soft HB or B pencil can be used.

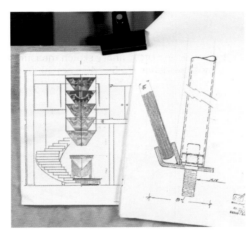

▲ Sometimes the design must incorporate the drawing for the supports that will hold the glass sheets and the space where the stained glass piece will be located.

▶ A prototype can be made with the material that the artist considers most appropriate. In this illustration, the prototype is made at a scale of 1:12, and poster board painted with watercolors and steel wire have been used. Because the design calls for using the collage method, the glass lines indicating lead came have not been included in the drawing.

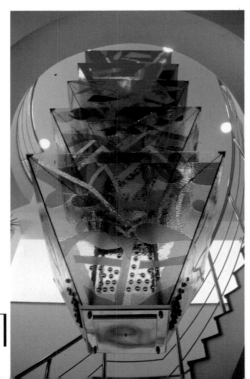

◀ The completed stained glass piece installed in the location for which it was designed, the lobby of a factory. Its full-size dimensions are 16 feet 8 inches high by 4 feet 8 inches wide (500 × 140 cm).

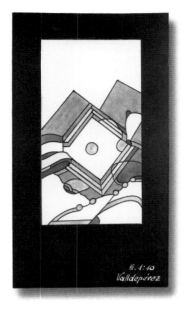

▲ The design serves as a model for carrying out the project, which in this case has been drawn to a scale of 1:12, using watercolors. The lines of the lead came have been drawn with black ink.

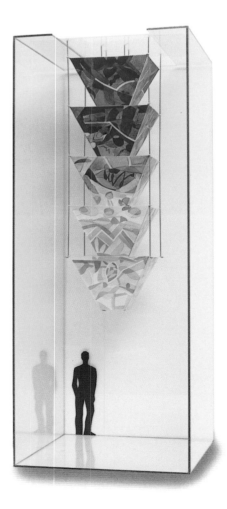

▲ Marc Chagall completed the sketch and design of some stained glass windows for a synagogue in Jerusalem. Shown in this photograph is the first sketch—6 by 8 inches (15 × 20 cm)—which he did with a thin brush, india ink, and pencil.

▲ The second preliminary sketch measured 11 1/2 by 16 1/4 inches (29.5 × 40.5 cm) and was done with india ink. The drawing and the wash were made with a small brush.

▲ In the first design, which was 6 by 8 inches (15 × 20.2 cm), he indicated color with watercolor paints, and he redrew the lines with india ink.

▼ Chagall did not make the stained glass window. The artists Charles Marq and Brigitte Simon from the Simon Studio in Reims, France, were in charge of its construction. The stained glass piece differs from the design that Chagall made for technical reasons, because he did not take into account the structure or the lead came. The lemon yellow background suggests that the stained glass window, which faces North, does not get much natural light. It was finished in 1961. Its actual dimensions are 8 feet 4 inches by 11 feet 3 inches (251 × 338 cm).

▼ Chagall prepared a prototype with gouache and a collage of colored papers; it measured 8 3/4 by 19 1/4 inches (22 × 48 cm).

▼ The final design of the stained glass measured 12 3/4 by 16 3/4 inches (32 × 42 cm) and was done with gouache and collage.

Full-Scale Drawing

The preliminary full-scale drawing that precedes production of the stained glass and that follows the design stage is referred to as the **cartoon**.

It is a good idea to use a medium-weight paper like the one used for these projects. In cases where grisaille will be part of the design, white paper should be used so the drawing will be clear. All information required for the construction of the stained glass should be noted on the cartoon: the lead came shapes and the variations of their gauges and thicknesses, the code numbers of the glass pieces, and so on.

The cartoon is also used for tracing the patterns or templates that will be used later for cutting the glass. A heavyweight paper should be used for making patterns.

During the Middle Ages, as well as now, the cartoon was used in the assembly of the stained glass. The cartoon is either placed on a table and the glass arranged over it, or the cartoon is placed to one side and the stained glass assembled directly on a table with the help of a carpenter's square.

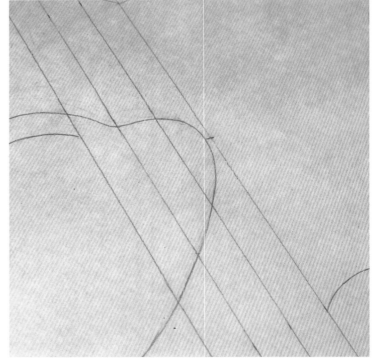

◄ **1.** The first step in the production of a cartoon or full-scale drawing. The design has been drawn to a scale of 1:12. Small variations from the design can be made to improve it or to clarify its details.

▼ **2.** A detail that shows primarily the outline or the width of the stained glass window. The outside line is the exact point where the stained glass piece should be placed. The inside parallel line corresponds to the glass. The overall pattern should be reduced by 1/4 inch (6 mm) to be able to wrap the perimeter with 1/4-inch lead came and to allow a 1/8-inch (4-mm) tolerance on each side.

▼ **3.** A detail of how to draw a line for the lead came so it is clear, without crossing other lines. A small space should be left between the lines, depending on the thickness of the lead came that the artist wishes to use. The drawn lines should be clear and well defined to make it easy to trace.

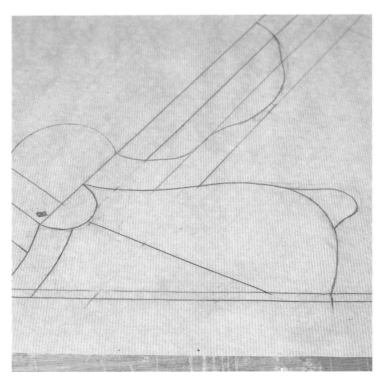

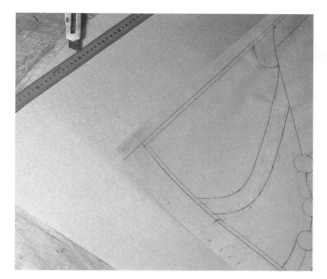

◄ **5.** Next, carbon paper is placed over the heavy paper, with the marking side facing down. To trace a mirror image, the carbon paper is placed facing up with the heavy paper over it, so the drawing will be reversed.

▲ **4.** When the full-scale drawing is finished, it is traced to make the patterns. To do this, a heavyweight paper, whose dimensions are slightly larger than those of the drawing, is placed over the table.

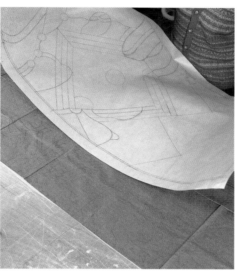

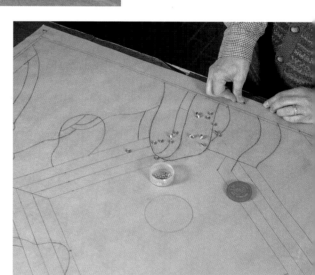

► **6.** Then the drawing is placed over the carbon paper, which should be big enough to copy the entire drawing.

► **7.** The drawing is held against the poster board and the carbon paper. Although thumbtacks are used in this case to attach it to the table, masking tape can be used if the entire drawing is to be transferred.

▲ **8.** The first thing to trace is the outline of the stained glass window or panel. Only the inside line is traced, that is, the one that belongs to the glass. It is advisable to use a hard pencil or a pen in a different color than the one used to make the drawing.

▲ **9.** Then, all the straight lines that can be made with a ruler are traced.

▲ **10.** Finally, the remaining lines are traced, always tracing along the center of the line where the lead came will be placed. This way, if the thickness of the gauge of the came is changed, it is not a problem.

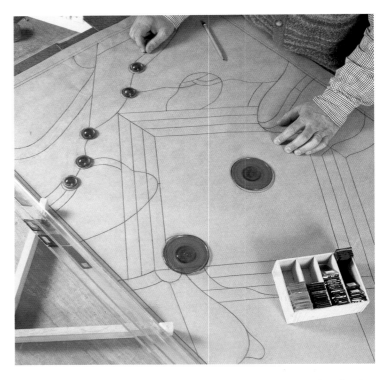

◄ **11.** Sample kit of the glass that will be used for the project. Notice that the top of each glass piece has a label: These references will serve as a guide for indicating the colors on the drawing.

◄ **13.** The pieces are pulled from the sample kit, and the colors that appear in the design are selected.

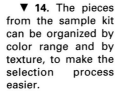

▼ **14.** The pieces from the sample kit can be organized by color range and by texture, to make the selection process easier.

▲ **12.** The selection process for the colors of the stained glass begins with the unique pieces, that is, the ones that are not referenced. Shown in the foreground are the spun glass pieces, the blown or molded glass pieces that are distinguished by their knob, which is the bulge or protuberance in the middle of the piece. Shown in the background are the glass jewels made in molds.

▼ **15.** Each time a color is selected, its reference must be noted on the drawing. If many glass types are going to be used, a consecutive numbering system can make their placement on the pattern easier.

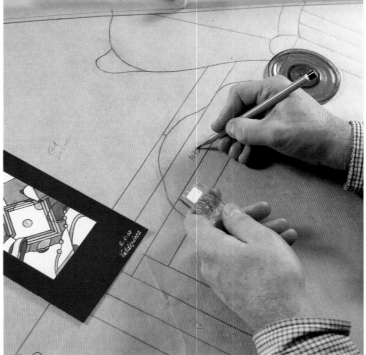

▲ **16.** After the colors of the stained glass are selected and noted on the drawing, the technical aspects of the stained glass piece are noted. In this case, a small curve is marked with a colored pencil on the corner of a right angle to remind the artist that it should be done this way when cutting the patterns.

◄ **17.** Then, the papers are separated. A corner is lifted first to make sure that the tracing has come out clearly. If it has, the carbon paper and the drawing are removed.

▶ **18.** The outline of the poster board onto which the drawing has been traced is cut out first. This can be done with a utility knife or with regular scissors.

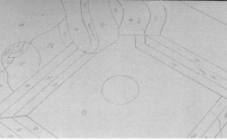

▲ **19.** Next, shapes are cut out with the pattern scissors. It is important to perform this step carefully, following the center of the line and taking care to make a continuous cut. Notice the small strip from between the shapes: This is the result of removing 3/64 inch (1 mm) from the outline of each template, which corresponds to the thickness of the heart of the lead came.

▶ **20.** After all the templates have been cut out, they are placed over the drawing to make sure none are missing.

How to Cut Glass

The great artisans of the Middle Ages used a red-hot iron awl to cut the glass. This way they were able to mark the surface of the sheet. Then, with grozing pliers they gave it the desired shape. Today, this process is much simpler because the technique has evolved and the appropriate tools have been manufactured.

In the following exercise, we explain the different cutting techniques, the appropriate tools for them, and the correct way of handling the tools. Keep in mind, however, that, as with any artistic endeavor, the artist acquires knowledge and good technique through practice.

► To store and organize the glass pieces properly, it is advisable to store them in wood shelves, classifying them by size and color.

◄ One of the many ways to hold a glass cutter is by placing the fingers as shown in the picture. This way the tool is held steady, becoming part of the hand. The part of the tool that has the small wheels must always be turned to the outside of the piece that is being cut.

◄ If you were unable to score the glass, try pressing the cutter, as shown in the picture. It is very important to keep the tool in an upright position.

▲ Roll the glass cutter across the surface while applying pressure on the glass. A sound similar to the rustling of cellophane paper and a small white line on the surface of the sheet indicate that the cut has been made.

▼ The glass cutting diamond must be held as shown in the picture. This cutter is used when the glass is very hard. The hardness is caused by the high quantity of selenium in its composition. In some types of glass, the diamond does not make any sound or white line. This tool is for personal use and should not be shared.

▲ The lubricated cutter, with a small wheel in a single head, has oil inside the handle. These tools are made with different shapes and cutters, and they are ideal for industrial cutting and for very thick glass. The cutter's shape allows it to be used in a tilted position.

▲ **1.** Beginning to cut a sheet of glass with some of the tools described. Using a grease pencil or a marker, mark the glass where the cut is to be made. It is a good idea to use a ruler to cut straight lines.

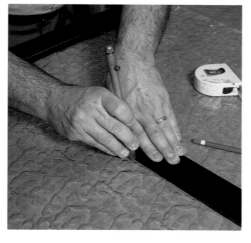

▲ **2.** The ruler must be moved slightly so that the small wheel will follow the center of the marked line. The ruler must be held firmly with the hand or some weights must be placed over it to keep it from moving.

▲ **3.** Place the fingers as shown in the photograph, and then carefully apply pressure on the sides of the glass sheet, in order to separate them. This will cause the glass molecules to break.

▶ **4.** The two sides of the glass are separated. Notice how both pieces of the glass have come apart along the entire scored line.

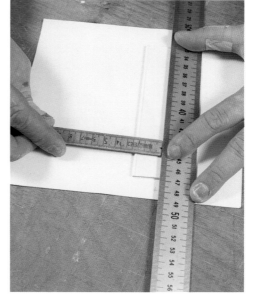

◀ **5.** In those cases where small straight strips of glass are needed, a glass template can be made to the desired size.

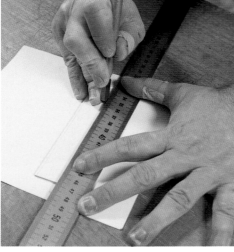

◀ **6.** After the dimensions are marked, the template is cut. Make allowance for the thickness of the wheel.

▶ **7.** The edges of the glass are smoothed with a diamond sponge or Carborundum stone to prevent them from cutting, and the shape of the template is adjusted to prepare for use.

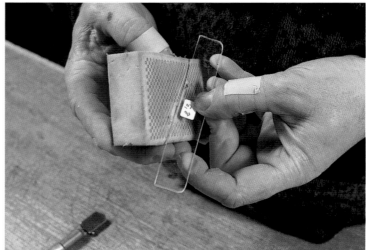

▲ **8.** Then, a metal gauge is set to desired dimensions. Keep in mind that the thickness of the wheel must be subtracted.

▲ **9.** Slide the gauge along the sheet of glass while holding the cutting wheel against the bottom side of the metal gauge.

▲ **10.** Separate the glass along the cut by carefully applying pressure with the thumbs.

▲ **11.** To cut strips of glass, the sheet of glass and the glass template are held against a ruler or a strip of wood that is thicker than the sheet of glass. Then, the wheel and the template are moved together along the surface of the glass.

▲ **12.** Using this method, strips of glass can be cut accurately and quickly.

◀ **13.** Glass of the required shape can be cut with a machine known as a lense cutter, which consists of a cutting wheel on the tip and a spring to hold down the sheet.

▶ **14.** The outline of the pattern is traced on a piece of glass with a wax pencil or a marker.

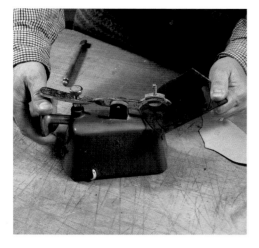

▲ **15.** Then, the glass is held with one hand while the wheel that holds the piece is turned with the other hand to cut it.

▲ **16.** Next, the cutting of right angles is explained. Begin with the most difficult part: the inside corners of the glass.

▲ **17.** First, cut off the excess glass. The pattern is held in place with weights.

◄ **18.** Finish breaking off the excess glass with pliers. Notice that the glass is rounded to better control the breaking.

► **19.** It is important to keep the pattern stationary; otherwise, the pieces will not fit when assembled later.

◄ **20.** Tap firmly and accurately with the glass cutter on the underside of the glass to separate the pieces of glass. The glass can also be smoothed out with the teeth of the grozing iron.

► **21.** Next, make the final scored line using the cutting wheel.

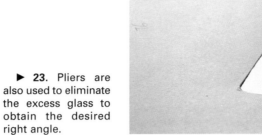

◄ **22.** Pliers are used to break off the remaining pieces.

► **23.** Pliers are also used to eliminate the excess glass to obtain the desired right angle.

▲ **24.** A ruler can be used to cut the outside right angle of the glass piece.

▲ **25.** The straight cuts can also be made with the help of a pattern.

▲ **26.** If the cut is accurate, breaking it apart is done easily and cleanly.

◄ **27.** Once the piece is finished, it is placed on the corresponding space in the drawing. Notice the accuracy of the right angles.

▼ **28.** A circle cutter, consisting of a central axis and a crank, can be used to cut round glass pieces.

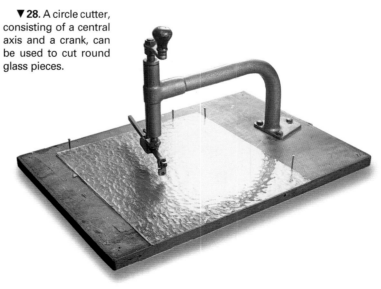

▲ **29.** Notice the point of the wheel and the central axis, which are used to increase or decrease the diameter of the circumference.

▲ **30.** Once the dimension of the circle has been determined, turn the wheel with the crank.

▲ **31.** A series of concentric circles is first made to weaken the glass in order to round it.

▶ **32.** Press gently with the fingers over the scored area to run the glass.

▶ **33.** To further open the cuts, tap gently with the scoring tool.

◀ **34.** Next, make a few radial score lines on the rings.

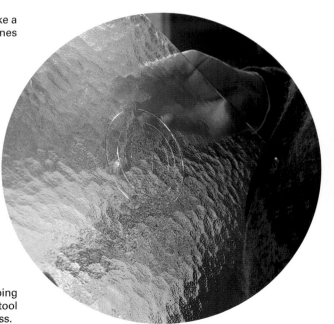

▶ **35.** Keep tapping with the scoring tool to weaken the glass.

◄ **36.** To make a hole in the glass, place a ball peen hammer under it, and tap the surface gently with another hammer.

◄ **37.** After several taps, a small hole will appear in the center of the circle, through which a grozing tool is inserted.

▲ **38.** The glass is chipped away with the grozing teeth, making concentric circles.

▲ **39.** Slowly and methodically, remove the concentric circles. Be careful, because a slight mistake may cause the glass to break in the wrong way.

▲ **40.** When the last circle is removed, the operation is finished.

► **41.** Next, with the help of a template, a cut in the shape of a half-circle is made in one of the corners of the glass.

◄ **42.** Remove the excess glass very carefully.

▲ **43.** To eliminate the tension in the glass, a triangular-shaped cut is made, in this case in the middle of the glass piece that is to be removed. Next, apply a few firm taps with the scoring tool.

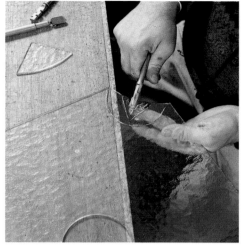

▲ **44.** Finally, remove the pieces of glass using pliers.

▲ **45.** Using a piece of glass as a knife, smoothe off the edges of the sheet so they will not cut.

◄ **46.** To cut a piece of spun glass, first check the diameter using a template.

◄ **47.** Using the template as a guide, cut the spun glass slowly, taking special care on the surface texture. To protect the raised area in the center of the spun glass, place it over a soft surface to cushion it.

◄ **48.** Remove the excess glass from the spun glass with pliers. If it is very thick, tap gently on the underside of the cut.

▶ **49.** To make a cut that has some degree of difficulty, use a grinder with diamond cutters. Mark the desired shape beforehand with a grease pencil or with a marker and a template.

▲ **50.** Check the line of the drawing to make sure it is clear, before the grinding is done.

▲ **51.** Remove the excess glass with a glass cutter.

▲ **52.** The pliers come in handy for removing the excess glass.

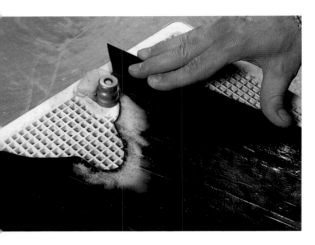

▲ **53.** Cut the glass to the marked line using a water-cooled grinder with diamond cutters.

▲ **54.** Place the pattern over the glass to cut the desired shape with precision.

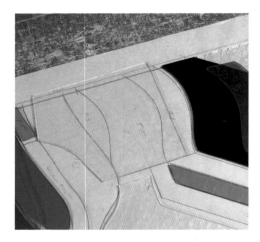

▲ **55.** To create a specific shape without using a template, place a piece of glass over the drawing of the required piece.

▼ **56.** Hold the glass in place firmly with one hand while scoring it with the other.

▲ **57.** The stained glass artist should slightly tilt the wheel toward himself or herself and proceed from bottom to top, in order to follow the line of the drawing with the tool.

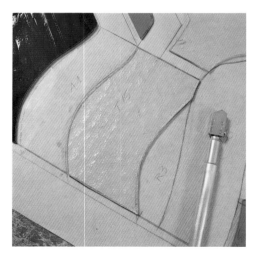

▲ **58.** Once the piece has been cut, put it on top of its place in the drawing. Notice that the cut has been made a little short of the lines so that it can be leaded at a later stage.

▲ 59. Place the templates over the sheet of glass in a way that minimizes waste of material.

▲ 60. Using a diamond cutter, cut the glass piece where the templates have been placed.

▲ 61. For a cleaner cut, it is best if the edges of the templates do not touch the edge of the glass.

▲ 62. Cutting should always begin with the piece that is easiest to remove from the group, in this case, the smallest piece.

▲ 63. Keep in mind the advice given in the previous step when cutting the remaining pieces.

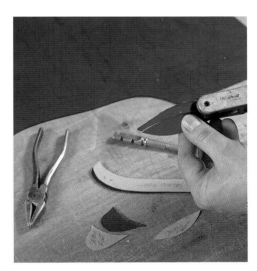

▲ 64. The separating of the different parts of the glass is done with the help of running pliers.

▶ 65. Once all the pieces have been cut and placed on the drawing, the placing of the lead came can begin, unless the glass requires painting. It is advisable to keep all the templates until the stained glass is placed in its final location, in case some pieces break.

Lead Caming

The properties of lead (softness, ductility, and malleability) make this an ideal material to work with. This is the reason why the first stained glass artists used it to support their stained glass windows. They drew their inspiration from Roman mosaics, like the ones from Ravenna and Pompeii, to create art that used pieces of glass instead of tessera.

Until the latter part of the nineteenth century, lead came in the shape of an **H** was the only type of support used for stained glass. Since that time, new materials have emerged, including copper foil, concrete, reinforced concrete, aluminum, different silicones and epoxies, and fussing. However, lead continues to be the material that is the most useful when it comes to making new pieces and when preserving and restoring old ones.

There are different shapes and sizes of lead came. The lead came used in the following exercises is 1/4 inch (7 mm) wide, one of the most common sizes. However, in the examples of the "Step by Step" section, different sizes are used, depending on the technical and aesthetic needs.

▲ Roll of lead of about 55 pounds (25 kg), as it arrives in the stained glass artist's studio from the foundry. Notice the channel that will serve as a guide for inserting the rollers.

▲ Different profiles can be obtained by using rollers of different shapes.

▶ Placing the rollers in the lead-stretching machine. There are small wheels in the two axles in the machine; they are the ones that produce the markings that appear in the channel. The distance between the wheels will be the width of the heart of the came, which is normally 1/16 inch (2 mm) thick. The marks in the channels are made to ensure that the glass stays in securely and to make the adhesion of the putty easier.

▲ Before the lead came is inserted in the machine, it must be lubricated with mineral oil.

▶ When the came is put through the reducing rollers, it gets thinner and the shape becomes more refined. The reducing step is done so that the lead does not become overheated while beginning to give it the required shape.

◀ To obtain the desired thickness, the appropriate rollers and wheels with finer grooves are installed after the reducing operation. The came can become three times longer than it was originally.

▲ The lead came is stretched by using a small T-shaped steel tool with a notch in the middle. The tool is attached to the table with a screw and the end of the came is inserted in it, as shown in the picture.

▲ Next, the lead came is stretched slowly, until the appropriate temper is achieved.

▶ In case the T-shaped tool is not available, one end of the came can be held with the heel and stretched from the other end with a pair of pliers until the desired temper for its use has been obtained.

▲ Required tools for leading the glass: a hammer, nails, lead knife or cutting spatula, lathekin, metal spatula, wooden spatula, pliers, and measuring tape.

▲ 1. Leading begins by holding a large piece of glass, which will serve as support for the others, with tapered steel nails. The nails are tilted slightly toward the glass to hold it more efficiently.

▲ 2. The length of the came to be cut is measured with the measuring tape.

◀ 3. Next, the lead came is cut. The cut must be clean and precise.

◀ 4. To fit the lead to the right angle of the glass, a mitered cut is made on both sides of the came. Notice how the edge of the glass stays inside one of the guides of the lead came.

▲ **5.** Finally, both lead came pieces are joined together, resulting in a perfect right angle.

▲ **6.** Next, a different method for lead caming a right angle is explained. The faces of the lead came at one end are cut and separated with a leading knife.

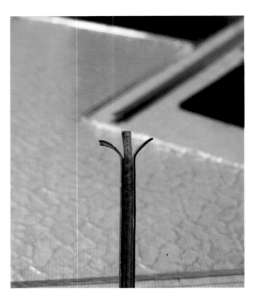

▲ **7.** Notice what the lead came looks like after the previous step.

▲ **8.** The piece of the came heart is removed with a pair of common or metal cutting scissors. The procedure is repeated with the piece of came from the other side of the right angle.

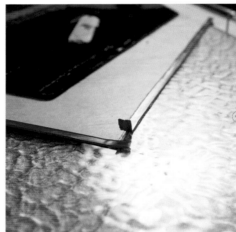

▲ **9.** The two pieces of lead came are slid along the edges of the glass until their faces overlap.

▲ **10.** Notice how the faces overlap.

◄ **11.** To protect the glass, a spatula is placed between it and the faces of the lead came. Next, with a leading knife, the faces are cut diagonally and the excess pieces are removed.

◄ **12.** Notice how the result is similar to the previous one. This procedure must be repeated on the bottom side of the glass.

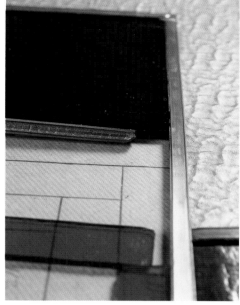

▲ 13. The joints between each of the various lead came strips that form the web of a stained glass piece must be perfect. This is one of the most important procedures of the leading up operation because it provides strength to the stained glass.

To join two pieces of lead came, first, a small wedge shape should be made on the end of the came, flattening the heart with a light tap of the hammer.

▲ 14. Then, the came is turned over so the wedge faces down in order to make it easier to slide.

▲ 15. The lead came is inserted into the channel of the other came with the help of a lathekin or a spatula.

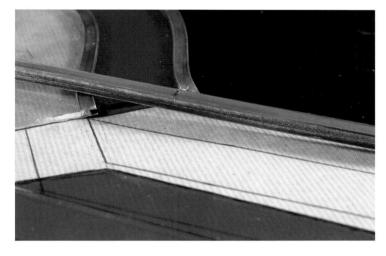

◄ 16. In this picture, one lead came is joined with the other.

◄ 17. To make an angle without cutting the lead came, first the came is set in place, and the point where it must be bent is marked.

▼ 19. Thanks to the incisions made on the lead came, it can be easily bent.

▼ 20. The glass is inserted into the lead came. Notice that the lines formed by the lead came lines are sharp and clean.

▲ 18. With the caming knife, a few small incisions are made on the faces of the lead came to allow them to overlap the end of the other lead came. It is important that the caming knife is well sharpened; otherwise it will crush the faces instead of cutting them.

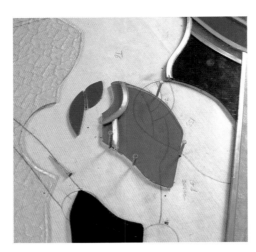

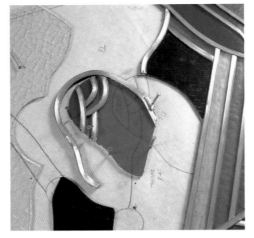

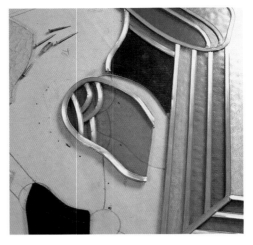

▲ **21.** In cases where lead came has to be applied to glass with complicated shapes, the following procedure can be followed. First, the main piece is held in place with nails, and then the smallest pieces are attached to it with the lead came.

▲ **22.** A scrap of lead came is used between the nail and the lead came strip so it will not be damaged when nails are used to hold a piece of glass that has already been leaded.

▲ **23.** Once the lead came has been placed on all the pieces, the assembly is carefully slid over the surface of the table to its corresponding place on the drawing of the stained glass.

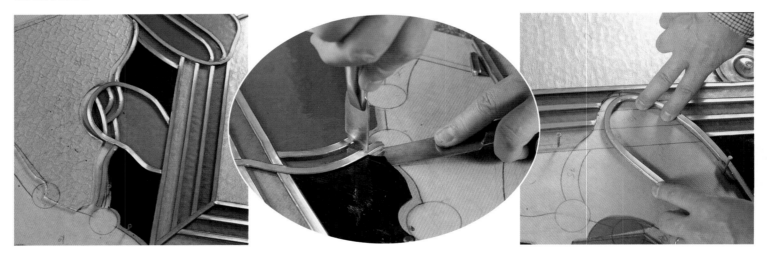

▲ **24.** Then, lead came is applied to the next piece of glass, and so on.

▲ **25.** Whenever the leading knife is used to cut off the ends of the lead came to insert them in the channel of another piece of lead came, a spatula should be placed underneath to protect the drawing.

▲ **26.** The photograph shows how to place a piece of lead came so that the ends of the other strips of lead came and the glass can be inserted in it. The lead strip is pushed into the shape of the opening.

▶ **27.** After the lead came has been put in place, it is held there with a nail, protecting the faces of the came with a piece of lead came scrap.

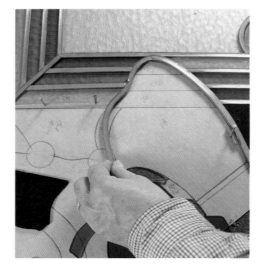

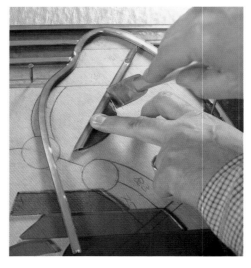

◀ **28.** To insert a piece of glass in a space that is surrounded by lead came, first the piece itself should be leaded. To do this, a strip of lead came is slid over the edge of the glass; the excess came is removed with a leading knife.

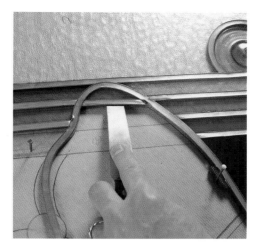

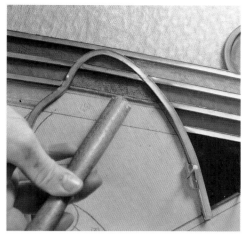

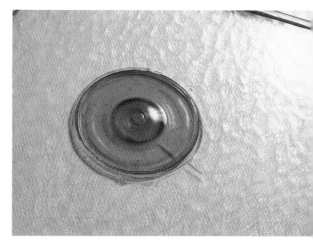

▲ **29.** The ends are flattened to make good joints, and the piece is put in its place with a spatula.

▲ **30.** Then, the next piece of glass is inserted. To make sure that it fits perfectly into the lead came, a few light taps are applied with the handle of the hammer.

▲ **31.** Now a piece of spun glass will be inserted into another piece of glass.

▼ **32.** First, a strip of lead came is placed around the piece to measure its length.

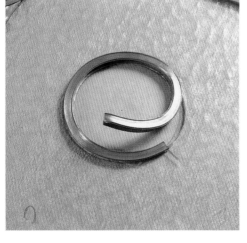

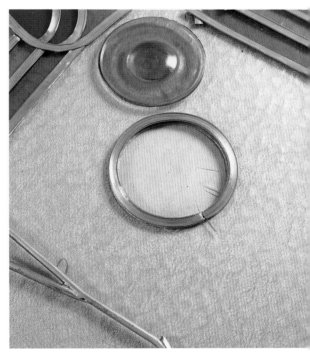

▲ **33.** Next, the lead came is cut and placed around the edges of the opening in the glass.

▶ **34.** The ends can be cut off to make the piece of lead came fit perfectly.

◀ **35.** Part of the edge of the face is lifted with a lathekin until it is vertical. This way, enough space is opened to allow the spun glass to fit in.

▶ **36.** The spun glass piece is inserted into the side of the lead came that has not been lifted. Then it is helped into place with a spatula until it rests inside the circle. Keep in mind that the protruding part of the spun glass should always face the top of the stained glass piece.

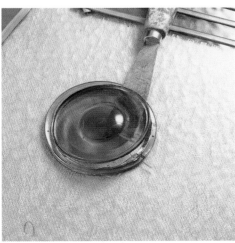

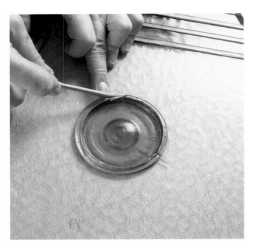

▲ 37. Once the spun glass has been fitted inside the circle, the face of the lead came is pushed back to its original position with a lathekin.

▲ 38. Finally, the lead came that holds the glass in place is rounded over with a wooden spatula to avoid scratching the glass.

▲ 39. To apply lead came to several rondels, a cylinder of a smaller diameter than the pieces can be used to roll a length of lead came to make as many rings as spun glass pieces.

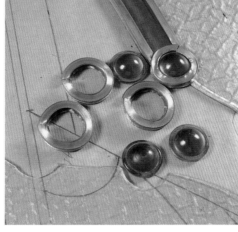

◄ 40. Next, the spiral is removed from the cylinder and a vertical cut is made with a caming knife to separate the rings.

◄ 41. Then the lead came is placed around the rondels and the pieces returned to the corresponding place in the drawing.

◄ 43. Next, the pieces are assembled, inserting the ends into the lead came that surrounds the rondels.

◄ 42. Before the assembly, the ends of the came already in place should be tapped with a hammer to give them a wedge shape. It is advisable to place a caming knife under the ends to protect the drawing while doing this.

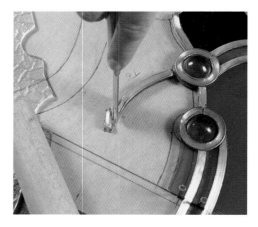

▲ 44. To connect one piece of lead came with another that has been cut at an angle, the end of the came is cut off following the curve of the rondel.

▲ **45.** Next, with a caming knife or a lathekin, the end is flattened to insert it into the channel of the other strip of lead came.

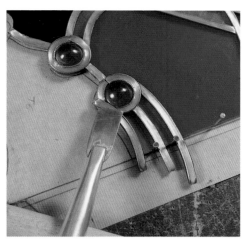

▲ **46.** The faces of the lead came pieces are pressed down with a caming knife so they will hold better.

▲ **47.** The joint of the two ends of the lead came that surrounds the rondel coincide with the connection of another piece of lead came. This way, the three ends will be joined with one soldered joint.

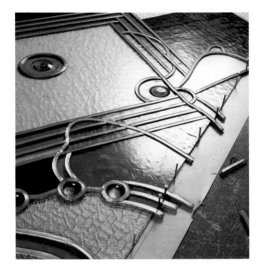

▲ **48.** The photograph shows how the outside of the stained glass piece is held in place with nails to prevent it from moving out of place.

▲ **49.** Once all pieces have been leaded, the excess came is cut off with a caming knife and the ends flattened.

▶ **50.** Next, lead came is applied to the entire perimeter of the stained glass piece. One way of holding the outside lead came in place is by inserting small pieces of scrap came between the nail and the lead came, like a wedge.

◀ **51.** Pieces of glass can be used instead of lead strips to hold the came on the outside edge in place.

▶ **52.** Similarly, a glass strip serves the purpose of holding the lead came in place while protecting it.

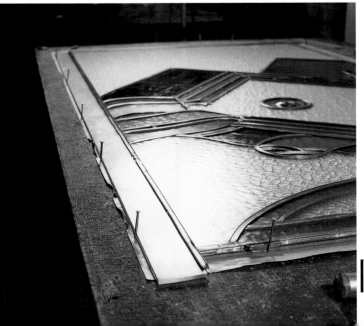

▲ **53.** Next, the lead came on the stained glass pieces is rounded over using a wooden spatula so the glass will not get scratched.

▲ **54.** A metal spatula can also be used; however, great care must be taken so that the glass is not damaged.

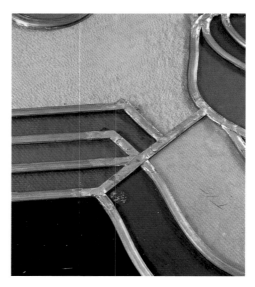

▲ **55.** Later, flux is applied to all the lead came joints.

◄ **56.** All the joints are soldered with an electric soldering gun and 55 percent tin solder in rod form.

► **57.** The solder applied to the corners should cover the entire surface of the joint to ensure a better connection.

▼ **58.** After this procedure, the stained glass panel is turned over. To do this, it is slid over the surface of the table until only half of the panel is on the table.

▼ **59.** Then, very carefully, the stained glass is held in an upright position, guided with the hands, and laid on its other side over the surface of the table.

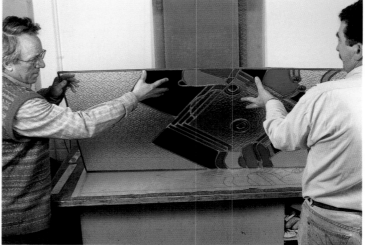

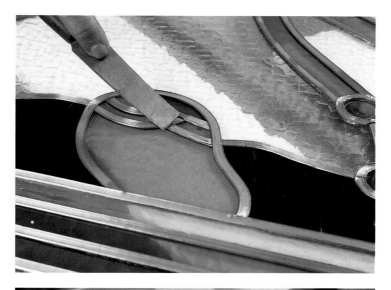

◄ **60.** The lead came of the reverse side of the stained glass is rounded over, this time with a metal spatula. To protect the raised areas of the rondels and the glass beads, a soft material about 1/2 inch (1 cm) thick is placed under them.

► **61.** The joints of the lead came are brushed with flux.

◄ **62.** The joints are soldered with an electric soldering gun and 55 percent tin solder.

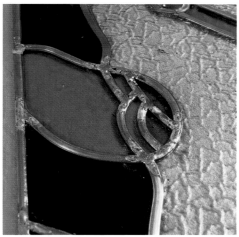

► **63.** The solder has run over the surface of the lead came.

▼ **66.** The lead came not only functions as a framework but also adds to the beauty, because it shows off the shape and color of the glass pieces and emphasizes their texture.

▼ **64.** Detail of the stained glass. The artist has done a fine job leading up the corners.

▼ **65.** The spun glass piece has been inserted and leaded with precision.

How to Putty

After the leading up and the soldering has been completed, the result of the stained glass making process is apparent. Although the piece can even be installed in the place for which it was designed, the project is not over yet, because even though the lead came may be rounded over, it does not hold the glass firmly. Putty must be applied to create a strong, long-lasting structure that will prevent vibration and deterioration caused by the elements.

The traditional putty, or mastic, used by the stained glass artist is available through specialized stores. It is a paste made of a mixture of calcium sulfate and linseed oil, which adheres to wood and iron surfaces and acts as support for the stained glass, much like a strip of wood. It is very durable and water repellent, which is why it is used outside.

To make the stained glass watertight and airtight, the putty must be mixed with a dash of turpentine to help thin the paste to the requirements of the stained glass artist so it can be inserted easily between the lead came and the glass.

It takes 30 days from the time of application for the putty to dry completely.

◄ **1.** Before its application, the putty must be kneaded until a uniform paste that does not stick to the work table is obtained. The putty in the photograph has been tinted with a black pigment.

► **2.** The putty is pushed with the thumb between the metal angle and the stained glass.

▼ **3.** Using a very smooth spatula, the putty is again pushed into the angle, and the excess is scraped off. Used this way, the putty serves the same purpose as a strip of metal or wood.

► **4.** The putty is thinned with turpentine in a container. Next, the stained glass is water-proofed. Either a brush with plastic bristles or a wide paintbrush is used to apply mastic, following the direction of the lead came. The best way for the liquid to penetrate the faces of the lead came is by applying it using a circular movement of the entire arm.

▲ **5.** The putty has already penetrated the faces of the lead came and has even seeped through to the other side. This indicates that the filling is complete.

▲ **6.** It is best to use sawdust to dry and clean the excess putty.

▼ **8.** Next, the underside of the glass is cleaned.

▼ **7.** The corners, the surface of the lead came, and any glass that has lines or texture are scrubbed with a vegetable fiber brush, because it is more difficult to remove the excess putty in these areas. It is very important to eliminate all traces of the putty because once it dries it is very difficult to remove.

▲ **9.** The underside is cleaned the same way as the top surface. Before turning the piece over, a sheet of some type of soft material must be placed under it to protect the spun glass and the glass beads that have been used in the stained glass project.

▶ **10.** After 48 hours, the putty that may have come out of the came during the cleaning process is removed using a metal, bone, or wood awl.

◀ **11.** The glass and the lead came are cleaned on both sides with a cloth wetted with turpentine.

◀ **12.** The textured areas must be wiped thoroughly to remove any stains made by the mastic and oxidized lead.

▶ **13.** A clean cotton cloth is used to dry both surfaces of the stained glass.

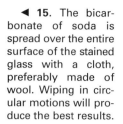
◄ **15.** The bicarbonate of soda is spread over the entire surface of the stained glass with a cloth, preferably made of wool. Wiping in circular motions will produce the best results.

◄ **14.** Bicarbonate of soda can also be used to clean the stained glass.

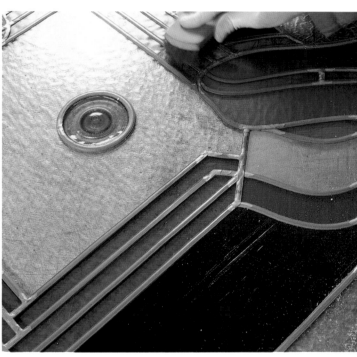

▲ **16.** The lead and the soldered joints are darkened by using a brush that is quite worn. Vigorously scrubbing the came and the solder will result in an even tone. This process will help conserve the lead.

► **17.** The stained glass project is complete after the previous step. Now it can be installed where planned. Its dimensions are 28³/₈ inches (72 cm) wide by 53¹/₂ inches (136 cm) high.

Patinas

During the nineteenth and twentieth centuries, architects, metal workers, jewelers, and stained glass artists, in attempting to reproduce the techniques and the materials used by artisans in the Middle Ages, developed a new way to make stained glass. This is how great artists and designers like Tiffany created furniture and lamps using the copper foil technique and patinas. Also, during the first part of the twentieth century, painting lead came in a gold color to imitate brass was common practice.

Although stained glass does not require a patina, because it is already beautiful, patinas are necessary to create different finishes to integrate the panel with the architecture or to give different qualities to the lead came.

The ingredients for patinas can be found in specialized stores. The following process will work with any patina formula. The patina used in this example has been made with copper sulfate, and has been applied over the tin solder, which was used to cover the lead came.

◄ **1.** Once the lead came is in place, flux is applied to all of the lead, on both sides of the stained glass.

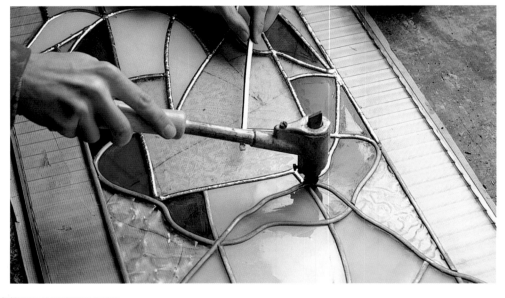

► **2.** The entire surface of the lead came is soldered on both sides with an electric soldering iron and 55 percent tin solder.

◄ **3.** Next, the putty is applied, because in this case the structure is made with lead came and not with copper foil. Once the putty becomes hard, the solder is cleaned very carefully with an aluminum or steel pad.

▼ **4.** Then, the liquid for applying the copper patina is prepared. The copper sulfate, which can be found in powder or crystal form, is dissolved in water until a cobalt blue liquid is obtained.

◄ **5.** The liquid is spread over the tinned lead came with a cloth, until the desired copper color is achieved. Rubber gloves should be used to protect the hands while performing this task.

► **6.** The excess copper sulfate is removed from the surface of the glass with a damp cloth or with a sponge.

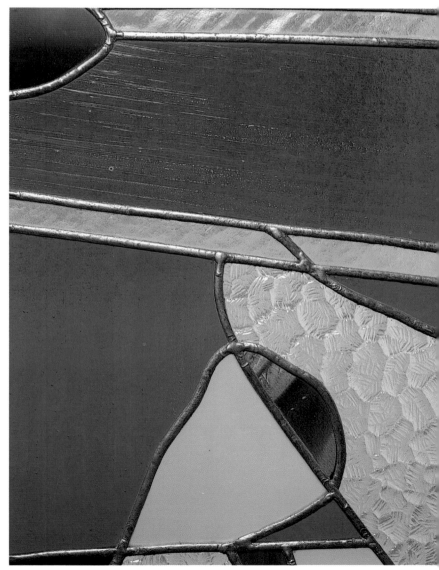

▲ **7.** The stained glass is dried with a clean cloth or sawdust until a shiny patina results. This process is commonly required on the other side of the stained glass.

► **8.** Final look of the copper patina. It can be cleaned with regular window cleaners, as long as care is taken not to scratch the surface.

ny type of craft work requires a learning process and some practice, to accustom the hands to carry out what the brain tells them to do. When perfect coordination is achieved, the apprentice becomes a master. Therefore, to master a profession it is necessary to practice, to experiment, and to make mistakes, learning from the errors themselves and trying to solve the problems with the resources available. The projects that are demonstrated in the following pages are a sample of the many technical possibilities and the array of materials available to the professional stained glass artist. The projects show that stained glass always goes hand in hand with the concept of light, but not necessarily with color. There is colorless glass that acquires its own personality if it is used properly. In the same way, the reader may observe that the structure of the stained glass piece transforms itself until it becomes one with the piece, contributing to the design and the form, or even becoming invisible to the eyes of the viewer. Therefore, in each step-by-step project, new aspects are introduced, whether technical or conceptual, so the reader may choose the one that best adapts to his or her needs and deepens his or her knowledge of the craft of the stained glass artist. This information is also complemented with a section dedicated to restoration, which covers the indispensable materials and techniques required to carry out the recovery and cleaning of an old stained glass piece.

Step by *Step*

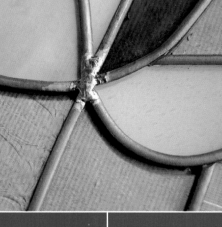

Stained Glass with Lead Came Lines

*D*escribed in this exercise are the steps for making a stained glass panel with a lead came whose round face is more rigid than usual. This type of lead came is very hard because of the rollers that have been used to shape it, so additional reinforcements are not required to strengthen the stained glass panel. It also fits together cleanly, so the panel can be placed in a location close to the viewer. This exercise also shows how to create a line using the lead came. This material, used primarily for support, can in this way play an important part along with the color and the shapes.

▲ **1.** Design of the entire project done in watercolor at a scale of 1:12. The stained glass is made of three panels, each measuring 25¼ inches (64 cm) wide by 77 inches (195 cm) high.

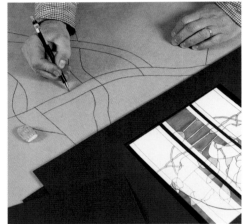

▲ **2.** The project is drawn at full size on medium-weight paper.

▲ **3.** Next, the drawing is traced using carbon paper.

▲ **4.** To indicate the changes in the thickness of the lead came, lines are drawn with different colored pencils with soft leads.

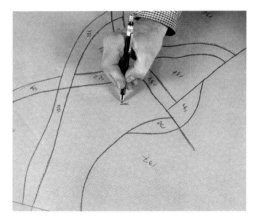

▲ **5.** The different types of glass used are also indicated on the drawing with numbers.

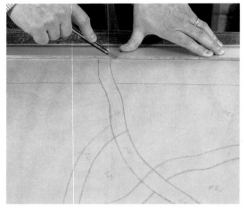

▲ **6.** The outside shape is cut with common scissors or with a utility knife.

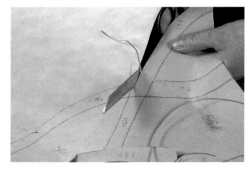

◄ **7.** The patterns or templates of the different glass pieces that will be used are cut with pattern shears. Thin strips of paper are cut away from the templates to allow for the lead came.

▶ **8.** It is a good idea to place the patterns over the drawing to make sure there are none missing.

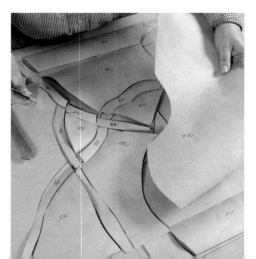

▲ **9.** The glass is cut with a glass cutter using the pattern as a guide.

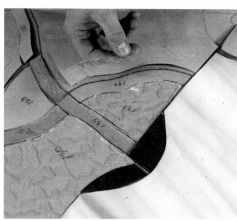

▲ **10.** The pieces of cut glass are placed over the drawing. When the stained glass is complete, the lead caming process begins.

▲ **11.** The round face lead came is known for its rigidity.

▲ **12.** To join the two pieces of lead came, a wedge must be made, cutting off the top and bottom parts of the lead (with a came knife or spatula) at the end of the piece that is to be inserted.

▲ **13.** Next, the pieces are put together and are soldered with tin solder.

◀ ▼ **14. and 15.** Join a $^3/_{16}$-inch (5-mm) lead came with another one $^1/_2$ inch (10 mm) wide by sliding the second one through the space between the two pieces of glass.

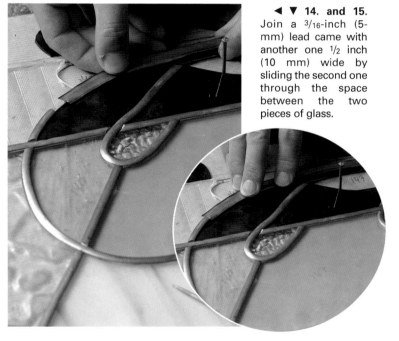

▼ **16.** After marking the length and the direction of the lead came on the glass, the face of the lead came is cut with a pair of scissors and the thickness of the heart is removed.

▲ **17.** The glass is cleaned with alcohol to remove the grease line.

▶ **18.** Multipurpose glue is applied to the face of the lead came, and it is bonded to the glass.

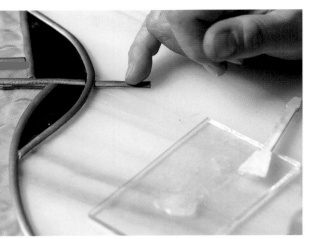

▲ 21. The solder is heated with the soldering iron until it melts and the face of the lead came is connected to the rest of the piece.

▲ 19. The lead came is adjusted and pressed gently on to the surface with a finger, all the while being sure not to dirty the glass.

▲ 20. For a strong bond, the face of the lead came must be soldered to the piece of the lead it touches. Flux is first applied to it with a brush.

▲ 22. The caming and soldering process is finished.

▲ 23. The detail of this soldered joint shows how the solder has run over the surface of the lead came.

▲ 24. When the soldering is complete, the putty is applied. In this case, it is recommended to use a type of putty that is stronger than usual.

▼ 25. The putty is spread thoroughly with a flat brush, making sure it goes inside the faces.

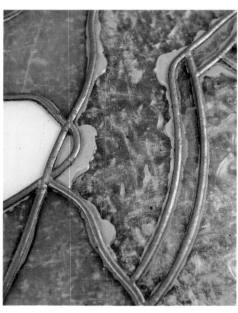

▲ 26. The putty is cleaned with sawdust, which also penetrates the lead came and, together with the putty, forms a dense paste.

► 27. The putty has traveled to the underside of the stained glass after it has been cleaned with sawdust.

▲ 28. The piece is gently brushed with a vegetable fiber brush so as not to remove the putty that holds the glass pieces in place.

▲ 29. After 48 hours, the putty is removed with an awl. The paste that is inside the lead came should not be extracted.

▲ 30. The traces of putty are removed from the stained glass panel with a small brush.

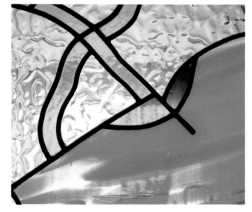

▲ 31. Detail of the lead came line over the glass.

▲ 32. Detail showing the different thicknesses of lead came.

▶ 33. General view of the group of three panels each measuring 25¼ inches (64 cm) wide by 77 inches (195 cm) high.

Panels with Industrial Textured Glass

*T*his project involves making a piece with glass panels that may appear simple but that have a variety of gray tones, shadows, and highlights, which Modernist and Art Deco artists knew how to use with great mastery.

It is very important to carefully select the glass pieces that are going to be used, because the result depends on it. This is why cathedral glass, acid-etched glass, flashed glass, and textured glass will be used. At the end of the project, it will be apparent that these materials are the most appropriate, even when the light comes through both sides.

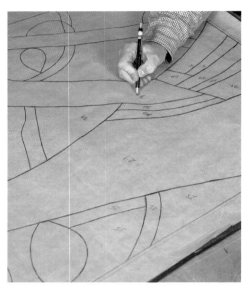

▲ **1.** This stained glass piece consists of four panels with symmetrical designs. Once the drawing of the two designs has been made at a scale of 1:12, the different glass pieces that are going to be used are indicated.

▲ **2.** Next, the scale drawing is converted to a full-size drawing, keeping in mind that the final size of each stained glass panel should be 35 by 74¹/₂ inches (88 × 186.5 cm).

▲ **3.** To make the templates, the drawing is traced with carbon paper onto poster board, and the glass references are copied onto it.

◄ **5.** The templates are cut with the pattern shears.

▼ **6.** Samples of various pieces of industrial glass, illustrating different highlights and gray tones, as well as the translucency of the glass.

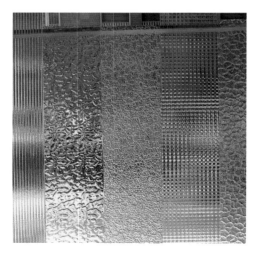

◄ **4.** The drawing and the carbon paper are pulled back to make sure that no detail has been left off of the poster board or the templates.

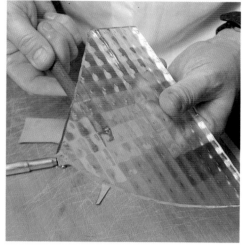

▲ **7.** The glass pieces are selected for cutting. The template is placed over the glass and it is scored with a glass cutter. This procedure must be carried out with patience in order to score across the textures in the glass.

▲ **8.** Sometimes, the glass, which is usually 1/8 inch (4 mm) thick, has to be tapped firmly to run at the cut.

▲ **9.** Pliers should be used to apply pressure to the cut to break the glass.

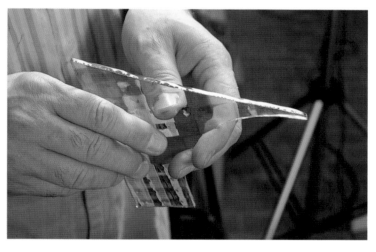

▲ **11.** The irregularities of the surface can be observed by looking at the edge of the piece of glass.

▲ **10.** When the pieces are large enough, another method of separating the pieces is by applying pressure with the fingers.

◀ **12.** The top and bottom edges of the glass piece are smoothed out to make it easier to insert it into the channel of the lead came.

▶ **13.** Notice how smooth the edges of the glass are.

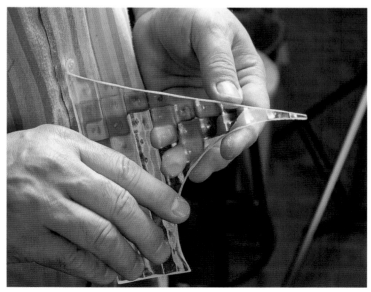

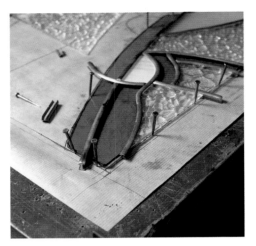

▲ 14. The lead caming process begins, starting at one corner of the drawing. For this project, 3/16-inch (5-mm) round headed lead came is used.

▲ 15. To remove the excess lead came, the drawing is protected with a spatula and the lead came is cut at an angle with the caming knife.

▲ 16. Next, to insert the glass, the lead came channel is prepared. After insertion, the lead came is flattened to hold the glass in place.

◄ 17. All the glass pieces are leaded, and then tin solder is applied over all of the came so a copper patina can later be applied.

► 18. The stained glass is turned over to solder the other side. To turn it over, the stained glass panel is slid across the table to its edge and then lowered gradually.

▼ 19. The stained glass is turned over very carefully, and it is again placed on the table.

▼ 20. The other side is soldered.

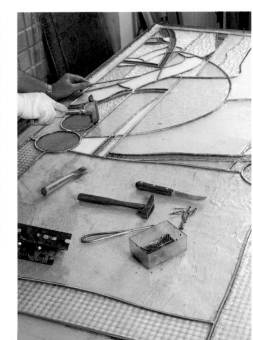

▲ 21. After both sides have been leaded and soldered, putty is applied. The putty should have a thicker consistency than that used for flat lead came, because it will be easier to insert.

▲ 22. The putty is cleaned with sawdust.

◄ 23. All corners are cleaned thoroughly with a brush.

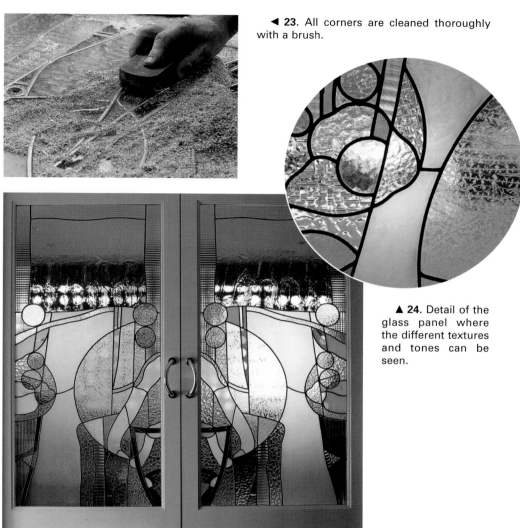

▲ 24. Detail of the glass panel where the different textures and tones can be seen.

► 25. Partial view of the stained glass panels placed in sliding doors.

▼ 26. View of the group of panels. The outside panels are stationary pieces and the other two make up the sliding doors in the middle.

Arched Panel with Antique Glass

*B*lown glass is known as antique glass because of the process used to manufacture it, which is the same process that glass artists used in the old days. Thanks to their hand craftsmanship, certain effects are achieved that other types of glass do not have, such as transparency with ridges, streaks, and bubbles, and a wide range of colors that allow more design possibilities.

Although normally used in large spaces such as cathedrals because of its color intensity, the example shown in this section was designed for the entry hall of a single-family house. It attempts to integrate in the stained glass the objects and the colors that decorate the room—and even the people who live in the house. The work done with the lead lines in the trunks of the trees reinforces the twisting movement in the design.

▲ **1.** Design done in watercolor and black ink at a scale of 1:12. Full-scale dimensions are 70 inches (177.5 cm) wide by 94 inches (238 cm) long.

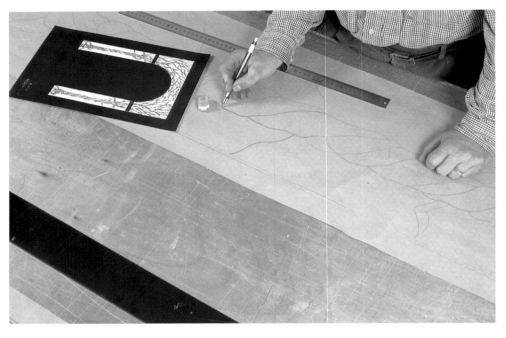

▲ **2.** Making the full-scale drawing from the plan done at a scale of 1:12.

◀ **3.** To make the pattern or the templates, first spread out a heavy sheet of paper, followed by a sheet of carbon paper, and then the drawing that is to be copied.

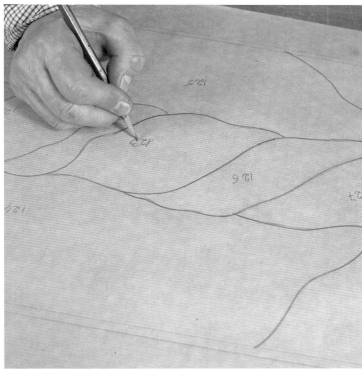

▲ **4.** Next, the drawing is traced with a pencil or pen of a different color than the one used before so that the lines that have not been traced yet can be easily identified.

▲ **5.** Then, the pieces should be numbered, using either a system that has consecutive numbers or a system that references the colors.

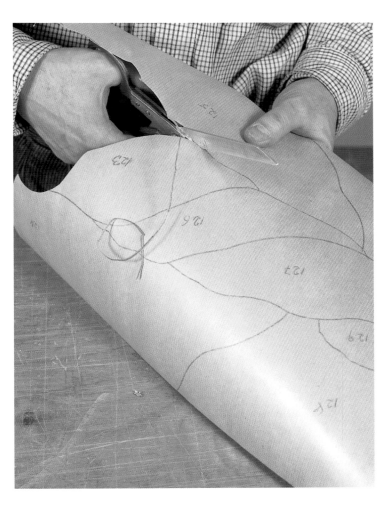

◄ **6.** Pattern shears, which remove the thickness of the heart of the lead came, should be used to cut the templates.

▼ **7.** The templates are placed in their corresponding locations in the drawing to make sure that none is missing.

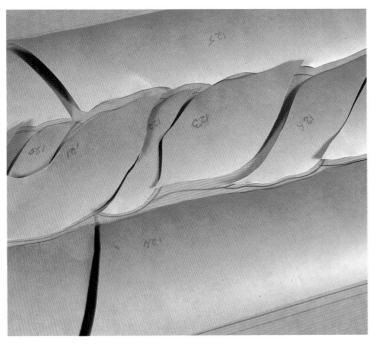

▲ **8.** The choice of the glass is extremely important in this exercise, because the irregularities in color serve a relevant purpose in the design of the piece.

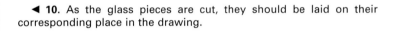

▲ **9.** To cut the glass, the corresponding templates should be used, positioning them in such way that there will be as little waste of material as possible.

◀ **10.** As the glass pieces are cut, they should be laid on their corresponding place in the drawing.

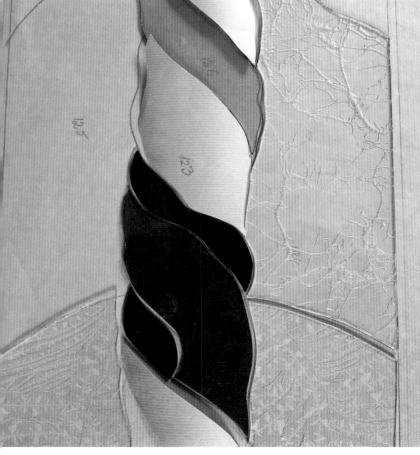

▲ **11.** Place the last piece of glass over the drawing. This is the best time to make sure that the result matches the design. If not, there is still time to change the colors.

▼ **12.** The next step is to apply the lead came to the pieces of cut glass. For the components of the trunk, it is advisable to use a lead came 1/4 inch (7 mm) thick. For the thinner parts of the branches, 3/16-inch (5-mm) thick lead came can be used.

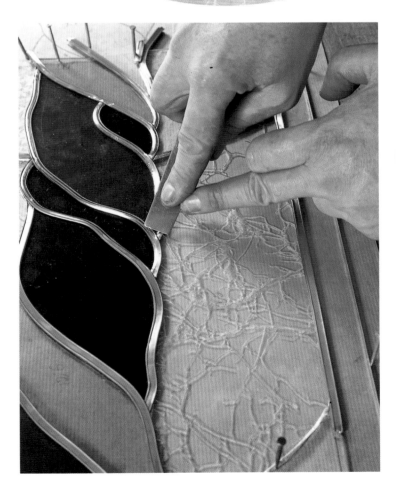

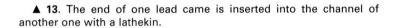

▲ **13.** The end of one lead came is inserted into the channel of another one with a lathekin.

◄ **14.** For the lead came to hold the pieces of glass firmly, the faces should be rounded over. This detail illustrates the movement that the stained glass acquires through the use of the helicoidal forms outlined with the lead came lines.

▼ **15.** Next, the lead came is prepared for soldering. The joints of the lead lines are brushed with paste solder.

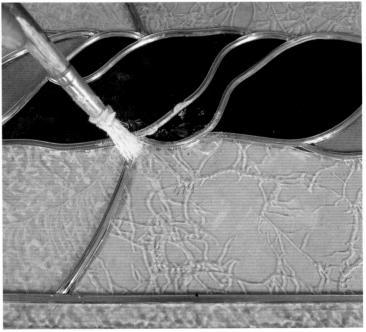

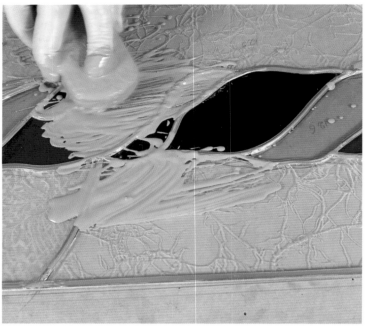

▲ **16**. The various lead came pieces on the top side of the stained glass project are joined with an electric soldering gun and solder. The process is repeated on the bottom side.

▲ **17**. The application of putty provides strength and firmness to the stained glass. The putty is forced into the lead came with a natural fiber brush, until the putty comes out on the other side.

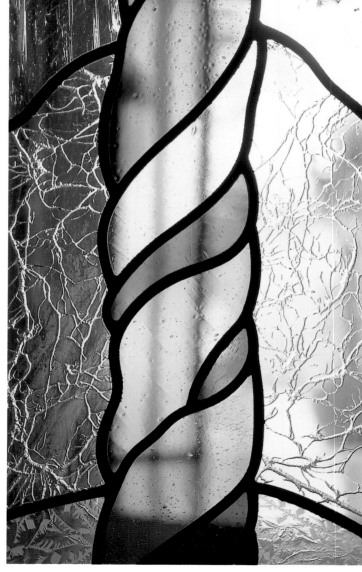

▲ **18**. The putty is cleaned with sawdust and a natural fiber brush; the corners of the lead came are gone over repeatedly. The lead came should be scrubbed thoroughly on both sides to achieve a uniform patina.

▶ **19**. View of the finished stained glass, installed in its final location.

▶ **20**. In the photograph on the opposite page, the delicate transparency of the glass, which highlights the hallway for which it was designed, is apparent. Overall dimensions: 70 inches (177.5 cm) wide by 94 inches (238 cm) high.

Stained Glass Window with Grisaille

*T*he following project was designed for the church of Aldover, a town in the Spanish province of Tarragona. This church is in a location that enjoys enough natural light to justify the use of grisaille.

The textures are what give value to stained glass painted with grisaille. In this case, the grisaille is made of copper or iron oxide mixed with borax, which acts as a solvent. The painting process is carried out on a light table, although to evaluate the stained glass window in its entirety, this process should be carried out in natural light and by bonding all the glass pieces with wax onto a transparent sheet of glass.

▲ **1.** Design of the stained glass done in watercolor at a scale of 1:12. The actual size of the stained glass panel is 22 inches (55 cm) wide by 53 inches (135 cm) high.

▲ **2.** A full-scale drawing of the design is made. The references of the glass pieces are indicated and the parts that will be shaded later are marked with a red pencil.

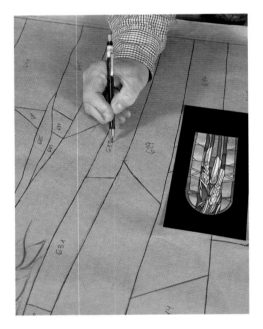

▲ **3.** The drawing is traced and the templates numbered.

◄ **4.** The original drawing and the carbon paper are removed, making sure that no line has been left off of the paper that will be used to make the templates.

► **5.** The templates are cut with the pattern shears.

▲ **6.** The different glass pieces are cut with a cutting tool, guided by the templates.

▲ **7.** As the glass pieces are being cut, they are placed on their corresponding places in the drawing.

◄ **8.** The glass pieces that are going to be painted are also placed over the drawing to be copied later.

▲ **9.** When all the glass pieces have been cut, they are cleaned with an alcohol-soaked cloth.

► **11.** The black grisaille that will be used to outline the designs is prepared by mixing iron oxide with pure wine vinegar.

◄ **10.** To select the most appropriate grisaille, a sample kit, which is prepared for the individual use of each stained glass maker, may be consulted.

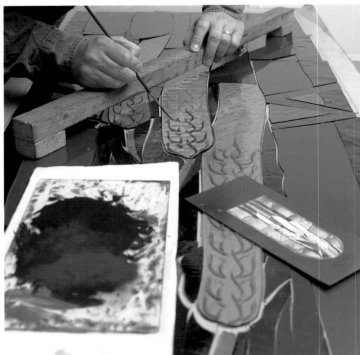

▲ 12. When the grisaille binds together completely, a few drops of gum arabic are mixed in to give the mixture a better consistency and to enhance its adhesion to the glass before it is fired.

◄ 13. The black grisaille is applied with a thin brush, using a bridge to avoid resting a hand on the glass and freeing the hands to retouch the lines. The drawing is left to dry for 24 hours. This procedure is known as *trait*.

◄ 14. The grisaille for outlining is prepared, which in this case will be brown (using copper oxide). It must be very fine and should be mixed with water because it is not compatible with vinegar. This makes it possible to paint it over another color without the need of firing it twice.

◄ 15. Bind the paste together thoroughly until a consistency is achieved that is neither too thin nor too thick.

► 16. A few drops of gum arabic are added to the grisaille as a fixative.

► 17. Over a light table, the brown grisaille is painted on the glass with a small brush.

▲ **18.** The grisaille is spread with a badger blender.

▲ **19.** When the grisaille is completely dry, the same badger is used to do the stippling.

▶ **20.** Using the bridge for support, the designs, or *enlevé*, are applied. To do this, the grisaille is "opened" with a small dry brush. This procedure can also be carried out with the point of the wooden brush.

▼ **22.** The *enlevé* technique is applied to different parts of the glass, this time using a very fine brush with a few hard bristles to draw the desired lines.

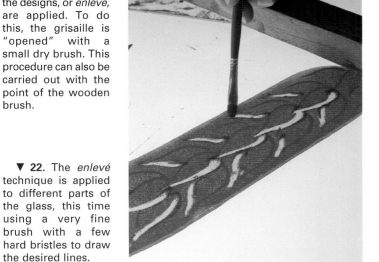

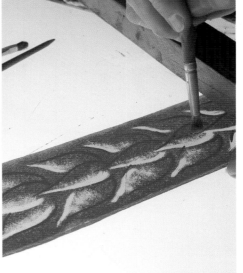

◀ **21.** The forms are modeled using the same technique, with a brush whose bristles have been cut flat.

▲ **23.** Texture is applied to the surface of the yellow glass using the same brown grisaille. For this procedure, a ball of crumpled newspaper is used.

93

▲ 24. The surface of the glass is painted as far as desired with a small brush.

▲ 25. The badger is used to cover the surface, blending the paint.

▼ 26. The grisaille is textured up and shaped with the newspaper ball, using it to absorb the paint.

◄ 27. Once the decorating process is finished, the pieces are arranged over a sheet of ceramic fiber in the top-loading kiln. The firing continues until a temperature of 1,112°F (600°C) is reached. Then, the kiln is turned off and left to cool.

◄ 28. The pieces are removed from the kiln and placed over the drawing to check if the desired result has been achieved.

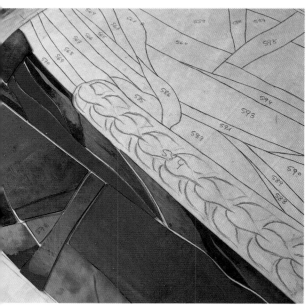

► 29. The lead came is placed around the glass, this time without the drawing underneath. The lead came is fitted to the glass by tapping with the wood handle of the hammer.

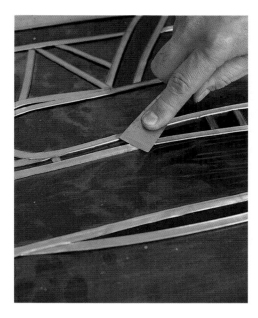

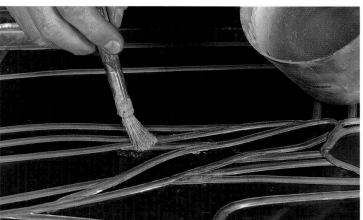

▲ **30.** Once the lead came has been attached to all of the stained glass pieces, it is rounded over with a spatula to fit it snugly to the glass.

▲ **31.** The lead came along the outside of the straight edges is held in place with a strip of glass. The curved lines are also held in place with small pieces of rounded glass.

▶ **32.** Flux is spread over the joints of the lead came.

▲ **33.** Next, the joints of the lead came are soldered with tin.

▶ **34.** When the soldering of one side is finished, the stained glass is lifted and turned over to solder the other side, after first rounding over the sides of the lead came.

▲ **35.** Once the soldering of both sides of the stained glass is finished, putty is applied.

▶ **36.** The putty is spread with a brush until it comes out on the other side of the stained glass.

▲ **37.** Sawdust is used to clean the putty and the stained glass.

▲ **38.** Sawdust is spread over the entire surface, paying special attention to the lead came pieces and their soldered joints.

▲ **39.** A brush is used to clean hard-to-reach places and to apply a dark patina to the lead came.

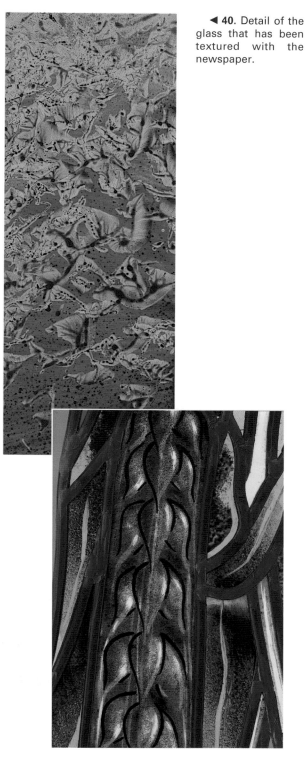

◄ **40.** Detail of the glass that has been textured with the newspaper.

▲ **41.** Detail of the glass pieces and their designs made using the stippling technique.

► **42.** Completed stained glass window.

Stained Glass Painted with Enamels

*I*n this project, enamel is used to emphasize the color range of the glass, which in this case will be cathedral glass. When designing a stained glass piece that will later be painted with enamel, the artist must keep in mind that this pigment lets a lot of light through, so an appropriate location for such a piece should be chosen.

Enamel is a paste made of oxides and minerals that is quite transparent. Its melting point in the kiln ranges from 1,022° to 1,076°F (550°–580°C), depending on the type of enamel used. Only black lets no light through. In chromatic order, blue and maroon have a higher opacity to light than yellows and greens.

◀ **1.** The goal is to make two stained glass windows for the staircase area of a private house. Of the two designs, done in watercolor at a scale of 1:12, the first is chosen to be developed in this step-by-step exercise. Each actual circular window has a dia-meter of 40 inches (102 cm).

▶ **2.** A full-scale drawing of the design is made on paper.

▼ **3.** To make the templates, the draw-ing is traced onto a heavy paper with carbon paper.

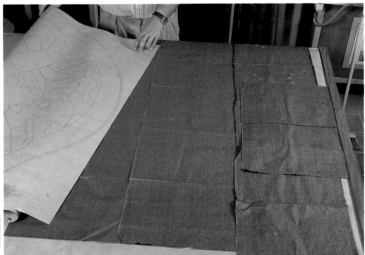

▲ **4.** The lines are retraced with a pencil to make sure that the drawing is copied on the paper.

◀ **5.** The glass pieces are numbered. Another option is to indicate the reference numbers of the colored glass sample kit.

▶ **6.** The drawing is separated from the carbon paper, and the lines are checked to make sure no details have been left out.

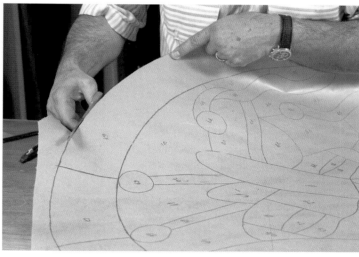

◀ **7.** The drawing is cut out with common scissors following its outside line.

▶ **9.** The templates must be cut carefully and with a steady hand, following the line, so the cutting tool can later trace the shape easily.

▼ **8.** With pattern shears, the drawing is cut following the lines that make reaching the center easier. The strips of paper removed by the scissors take away 1/24 inch (1 mm) from the contour of each piece of glass.

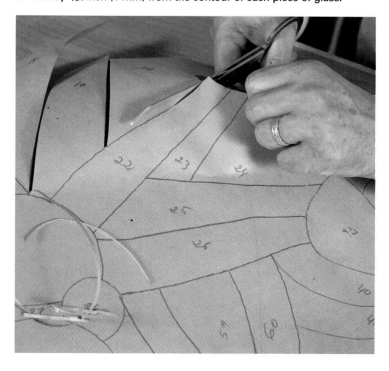

▲ **10.** Once the templates are finished, the glass is scored with a glass-cutting tool.

▲ **11.** View of the cut template and glass.

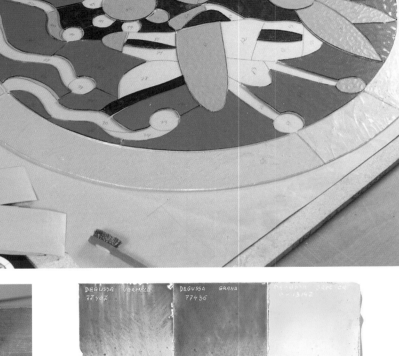

▶ **12.** The templates are removed as the glass pieces are placed over the drawing.

▼ **13.** Before the glass is painted, it must be cleaned with alcohol to remove any traces of grease and to allow the enamel to adhere properly.

▲ **14.** Samples of colored enamels that are made by the stained glass artist and used for painting.

▶ **15.** Next, the maroon enamel that will be used to paint the background of the stained glass is prepared. The paste can be mixed with turpentine, vinegar, or water. In this case, water is used.

◀ **16.** The paste is mixed very carefully with a spatula, removing the small lumps that may form. The mixture should be neither too thin nor too thick.

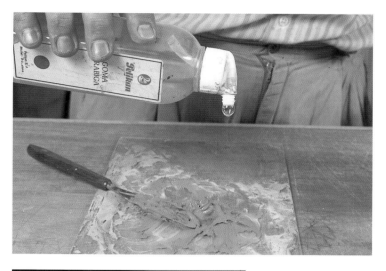

◄ **17.** When the mixture is almost ready, a few drops of gum arabic are added to it to help it adhere to the enamel.

► **18.** The glass is painted with a small brush on a light table to gauge the amount of color.

◄ **19.** A badger is used to remove the marks of the brush strokes.

► **20.** If a light table is not available, natural light can be used.

▲ **21.** The badger can be used to spread the enamel with more precision.

► **22.** The pieces are carefully put back in their places so as not to touch the painted glass with the fingers.

◄ **23.** The steel trays are prepared to fire the glass. First, powdered, dehydrated plaster is spread over the entire surface of the tray.

► **24.** A sheet of glass is used to press the layer of plaster to make its surface smooth and to pack it firmly.

► **25.** Next, the glass pieces are carefully placed on the plaster surface, taking up the least possible space and keeping dust from getting on them, because the dust would adhere to the enamel and cause an opaque stain.

▼ **27.** When the kiln is completely cold, the plate with the glass pieces is taken out and checked to make sure that the results are satisfactory.

▲ **26.** The tray with the glass pieces is inserted in the cold kiln and fired until a temperature of 1,076°F (580°C) is reached. The kiln is turned off and left to cool down.

◄ **28.** The glass pieces are placed on the assembly table and a ¼-inch- (7-mm)-wide lead came is applied to them. The process begins at the outer ring to ensure proper support.

▲ **29.** The excess lead came is cut off with a spatula.

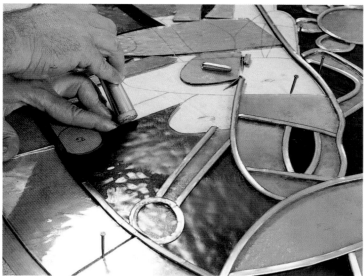

▲ **30.** The glass pieces are pushed into place and tapped lightly with the handle of the spatula, using the drawing underneath them as a guide.

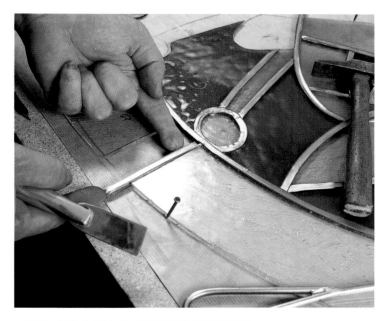

◄ **31.** The outer ring and the inside pieces are all leaded at the same time to ensure a better fit.

► **32.** The lead came for the outside should be 5/16 inch (10 mm) wide. It is held in place with pieces of scrap glass to prevent it from moving.

◄ **33.** The joint of the lead came around the outside of the panel should be made to coincide with one of the crossing lines so all three joints can be soldered together.

► **34.** Once the lead caming procedure is finished, the came is rounded over. Next, flux is brushed on the joints.

◀ **35.** The lead came is soldered.

▶ **36.** Once the stained glass has been soldered on both sides, putty is applied.

▼ **37.** The putty is spread with a brush. The direction of the brush strokes should always be perpendicular to the direction of the lead came, so the putty penetrates the came properly.

▲ **38.** Putty is brushed on vigorously until it comes out on the other side of the stained glass.

▼ **39.** Next, the putty is cleaned off with sawdust, paying special attention to the lead came and the soldered joints.

▼ **40.** The corners and hard-to-reach places of the stained glass are cleaned with a vegetable fiber brush or plastic brush.

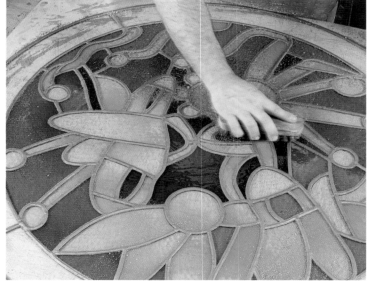

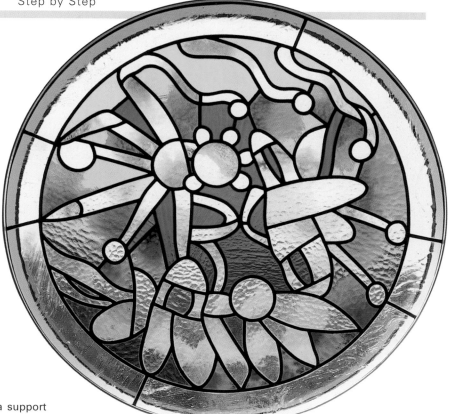

▲ 41. The putty is removed from the outside of the lead came with an awl or lathekin so it does not dry out and adhere to the glass.

▶ 42. To install the stained glass, it must be placed on a support structure made of aluminum.

▶ 43. View of one of the stained glass windows after it has been installed. Notice the reflection of the design on the interior stairs of the house.

Stained Glass with Copper Foil

*T*his step-by-step exercise shows how to make a pyramid-shaped stained glass piece using the technique that Louis Comfort Tiffany developed. This important American artist and designer, who lived between the nineteenth and twentieth centuries, introduced the copper foil technique, which replaced lead came as the support for the various glass pieces that form the stained glass. In this project, the pyramid sculpture is made of glass pieces that create various combinations of colors when light passes through two sides.

What is achieved with this technique? The weight of the stained glass is reduced significantly. The piece is more rigid than if it were done with lead came, because it is covered with solder. The line width can be reduced to $1/16$ inch (2 mm). Also, the infrastructure required to create a piece with this technique is minimal.

► **1.** Mock-up done in paper and watercolor at a scale of 1:5. The full-size dimensions of each triangle are 12 inches (30 cm) at the base by 18 inches (45 cm) high.

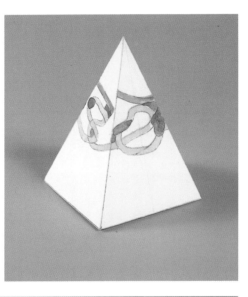

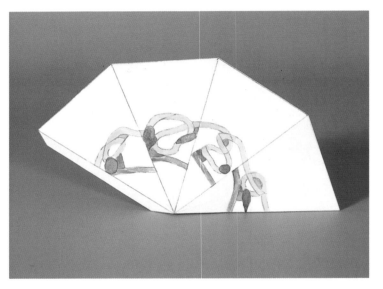

▲ **2.** The same mock-up unfolded. Notice that each triangle has a different design, which continues on the next triangle. The tab on the left side is used to join two sides of the pyramid model.

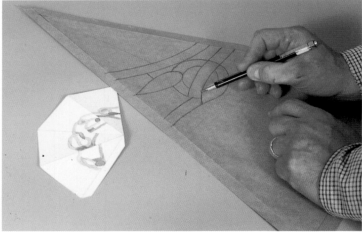

▲ **3.** To draw each triangle to full size, it is best to work with the mock-up unfolded. This will make transferring all the lines from the piece to paper much easier.

► **4.** Next, the patterns, or templates, of the four sides are traced. For this procedure heavy paper, carbon paper, thumbtacks to hold them in place, a hard lead pencil of a different color than the one used for the drawing, a ruler, and a cutting blade are needed.

▲ **5.** First, the heavy paper that will be the template is placed on top of the worktable. Next, it is covered with the carbon paper, inked side facing down, which in turn is covered with the drawing that is to be traced.

▲ **6.** The drawing is traced by pressing firmly to ensure that the best possible copy of the image is achieved. The outline of the outside of the drawing should also be traced.

◄ **7.** Next, the parts are numbered with the color reference or with consecutive numbers.

▼ **8.** Then, progress is checked to make sure that the tracing has come through clearly.

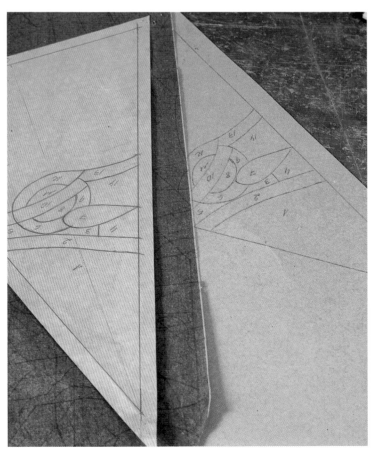

◄ **9.** The drawing is cut along the outside line with a blade and a ruler. To cut the various parts that make the template, pattern shears are used.

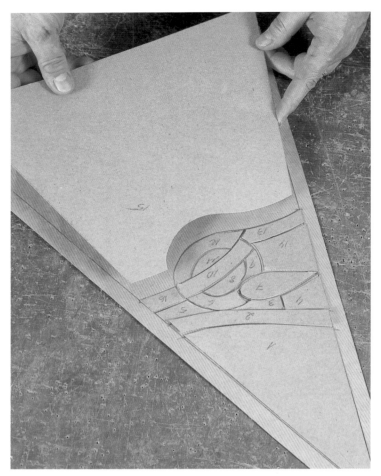

◀ **10.** As the pieces of the pattern are cut, they are placed in their respective places on the drawing.

▼ **11.** Next, the colors are selected. It is advisable to check the results of superimposing two glass pieces of different colors to get a third color.

◀ **12.** Once the glass pieces are selected, the cutting begins.

▶ **13.** The piece of cut glass is broken off with pliers. It is important that the edge be clean and smooth.

◀ **14.** It is a good idea to use a pair of running pliers to help break apart the two pieces of glass.

► **15.** The edges of all the glass pieces are smoothed with an electric grinder. This way, the adhesive on the back of the copper foil will adhere much more easily.

► **16.** Next, all the glass pieces are cleaned.

◄ **17.** All the glass pieces are perfectly cut and smoothed and placed where they belong in the drawing.

► **18.** The various pieces of glass are joined with copper foil. It is applied to the outside of each piece of the stained glass object. The copper foil comes in different widths that can accommodate the thickness of the glass. The 1/5-inch and 1/4-inch (5- and 6-mm) strips are suited for glass pieces 1/10 inch and 1/8 inch (2.5 and 3 mm) thick, such as the ones used in this project. It is best if the foil overlaps the surface of the glass 1/25 inch (1 mm) on both sides. As the picture shows, the edge of the glass is placed in the middle of the foil and attached by pressing on it.

◀ **19.** The foil should be pinched with the fingers at the corners of the glass pieces. Foil with a black reverse side is available, and it is ideal for a black patina finish.

▲ **20.** The copper foil should be applied slowly and very carefully to rounded edges so that it will not break. The foil should be folded over itself rather than cut.

▲ **21.** The copper foil should be pressed or "ironed" to the glass using a nonmetallic tool that is not too hard, like a dowel, a plastic spatula, or a piece of wood.

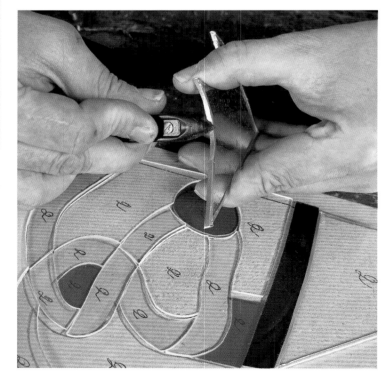

▶ **22.** The foil should be very carefully pressed to eliminate raised areas, which will make it difficult to join one piece to another. This is also done to ensure that the foil is bonded to the glass.

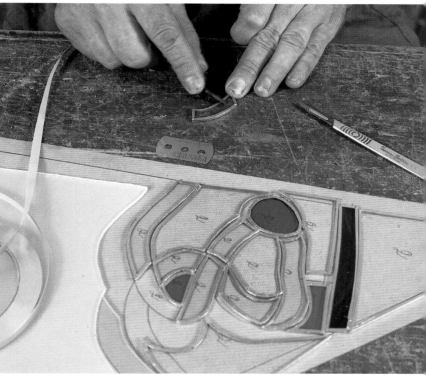

◄ **23.** The piece can be held in the palm of the hand for the smoothing step.

▲ **24.** The glass pieces can also be placed on top of the worktable. The irregular joints or sections of foil that are crooked can be corrected with a blade or a scalpel. This will result in a better finish.

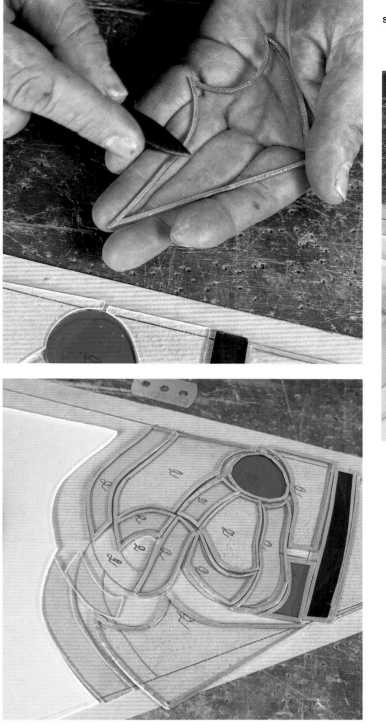

▲ **25.** Glass pieces with the copper foil placed back in order on top of the drawing.

► **26.** Once this step is finished, the soldering begins.

▲ **27.** For soldering, a triangular frame should be made with thin strips of wood to fit the glass panel.

▲ **28.** The pieces of one of the sides are placed inside the frame. The shapes of the pieces of glass and the copper foil can still be corrected if necessary.

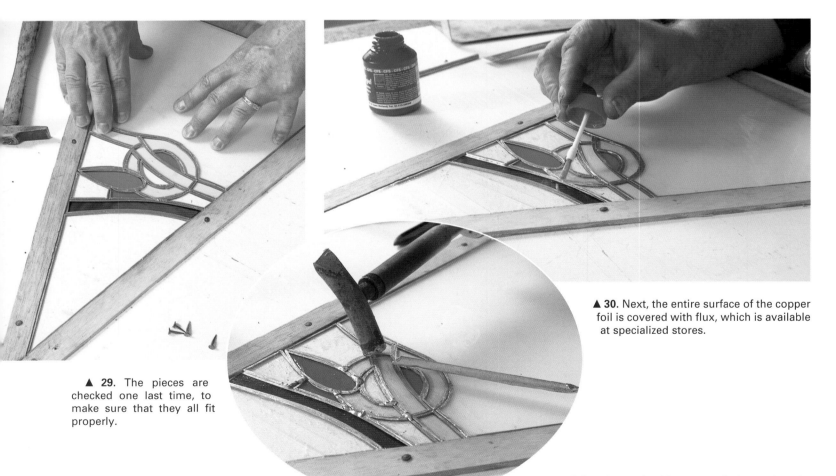

▲ **30.** Next, the entire surface of the copper foil is covered with flux, which is available at specialized stores.

▲ **29.** The pieces are checked one last time, to make sure that they all fit properly.

◄ **31.** A few drops of solder are applied, and then the pieces are soldered together.

▲ **32.** After making sure that the pieces are firmly held in place, the entire surface of the copper foil is soldered.

▲ **33.** Next, the inside face is soldered. This is repeated on each of the four sides of the sculpture.

◄ **34.** A small amount of solder should be applied to the border of the last triangle. This application will make it easier to join the different sides to each other.

▼ **35.** One of the strips of wood that was used to make the triangular frame is used as a stop to begin assembling the four sides.

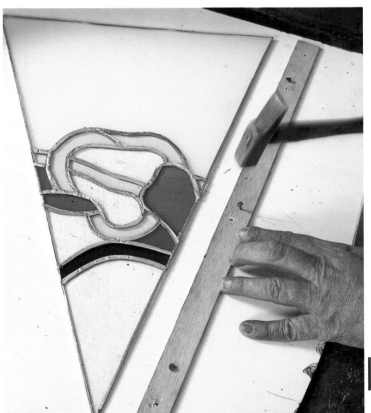

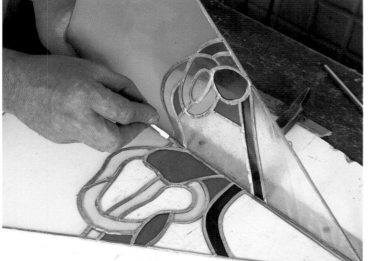

◄ **36.** To join two of the triangular panels, one is placed on the work table and the other against the strip of wood that acts as a stop, pressing on it and making sure the designs match as dictated by the model. Next, flux is applied to the pieces that need to be soldered.

▼ **37.** Before soldering, a few drops of solder should also be applied to hold both sides together.

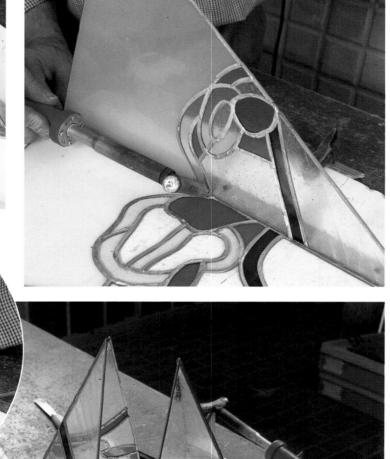

▲ **38.** Next, soldering begins with filling the gap created at the joint of the two triangles. Both sides must form a perfect right angle during this operation. The entire procedure is repeated on the two remaining triangular pieces.

► **39.** Moment before the final assembly of the pieces.

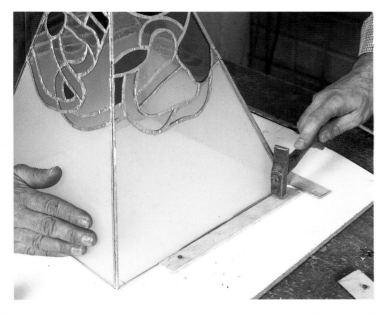

▲ 40. A stop is made in the shape of a right angle with two strips of wood, and the halves are joined together and adjusted as needed.

▲ 41. The same procedure is repeated, applying a drop of solder to the points where the faces meet, to achieve rigidity.

◄ 42. The top of the pyramid where the points of the four triangles meet is also soldered.

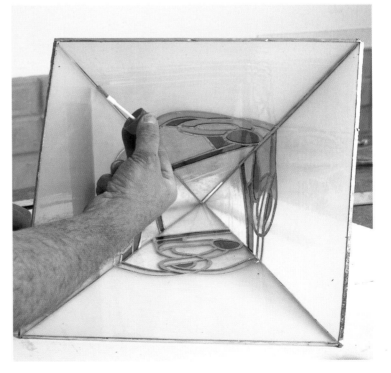

▲ 43. The pyramid is tilted and flux is applied to the joints on the inside of the stained glass pieces.

◄ 44. The angle formed by joining the two sides is soldered, filling the small gap that is formed. At this point, the base should be checked, to make sure it is perfectly square.

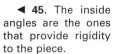

◄ **45.** The inside angles are the ones that provide rigidity to the piece.

► **46.** Once the sculpture is finished on the inside, flux is applied to the outside corners, which are then soldered. To make the procedure comfortable and to make the best use of the solder, the side to be soldered is placed on a flat surface.

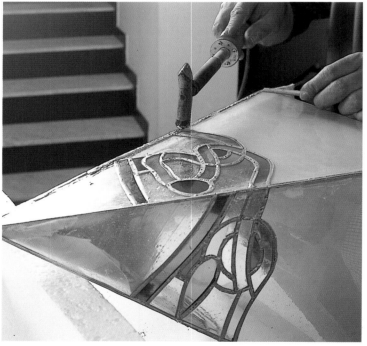

▲ **47.** A thin rod covered with a piece of cloth is used as a barrier for the solder so it does not flow to the inside when it melts.

▲ **48.** The cloth barrier is placed on the inside of the angle to be soldered. This step is repeated on the four edges of the piece.

◄ **49.** Next, the stained glass is cleaned with a product suitable for this type of material, which will remove the grease and the grime that accumulated as the sculpture was put together.

► **50.** Next, with a cloth dampened in copper sulfate, a colored patina is applied to the tin, rubbing until the reddish tone characteristic of this metal is achieved.

▼ **52.** In this picture of the finished sculpture, the transparency of the triangular sides and the elegant ensemble of lines and colors can be appreciated.

▲ **51.** Then, the surface is cleaned with a cloth soaked in water, until all traces of the copper sulfate have been completely removed. Finally, before the sculpture is considered finished, the pieces are dried.

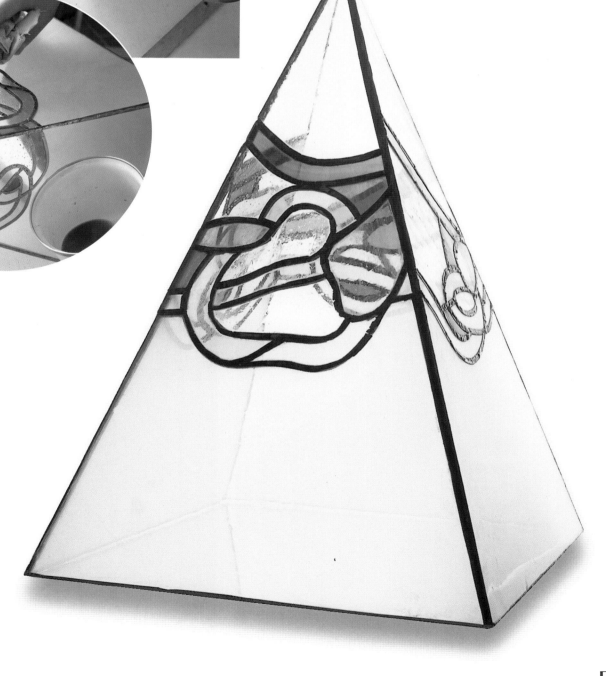

Stained Glass with Cement

W*hen making stained glass with a cement support, the cement is substituted for the lead came, which is the traditional support for stained glass. From a historical point of view, the use of cement with stained glass, which began in the first half of the twentieth century, has not yet been studied in depth.*

This step-by-step exercise explains how to make one of the most traditional cement and glass projects, a flat one, where the cement and the glass are of the same thickness. Dalles are used instead of the traditional sheets of glass, which are made by blowing. Dalles are made using the cast glass technique, forming hot glass in iron molds.

▲ **1.** Design of the stained glass done in watercolor at a scale of 1:12. Note that the thick, black lines correspond to the cement that will support the dalles. The full-size dimensions of the stained glass panel are 26 by 26 inches (65 × 65 cm).

◄ **2.** The full-size drawing is made. For the cement to flow between the dalles, a minimum of ³/₈ inch (1 cm) of space should be left between them.

▼ **3.** Two drawings are needed, so the original drawing should be traced onto another paper.

▼ **4.** The outlines of the dalles on both drawings are traced with a marker so they can be seen better.

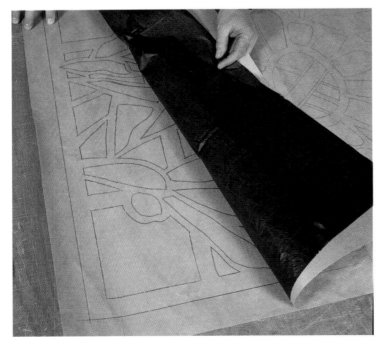

▲ **5.** Ink or clothing dye is applied with a small brush to the lines that represent the cement.

▲ **6.** This picture illustrates how the dalles are concentrated in groups.

▼ **7.** The dalles are numbered. One of the drawings is used to make the grid, that is, the structure that will support the cement and the glass. The rods, from 1/8 to 3/16 inch (4 to 5 mm) thick, must be made of stainless steel, because with time the panel could crack as a result of oxidation.

▼ **8.** These rods should surround groups of three or four glass pieces and must pass through the center of the areas marked in black in the drawing. They will be welded together using a resistance welder. To frame the stained glass, a border is placed—a piece of flat metal 3/4 inch (2 cm) high by 3/4 inch (2 cm) thick—around the perimeter.

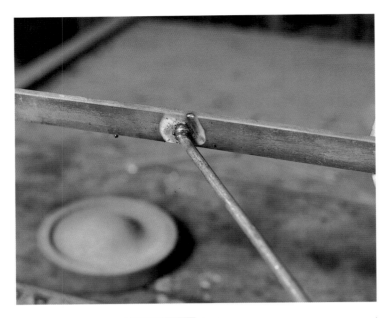

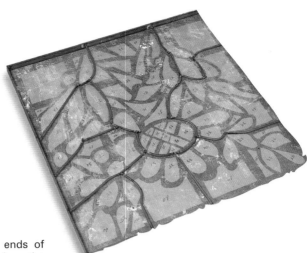

◀ **9.** The ends of the rods that form the grid should be welded to the edge of the frame so they will be covered when the cement is poured.

▲ **10.** Once the grid has been attached to the frame, a sheet of plastic is placed under the entire piece to begin setting the dalles and pouring the cement.

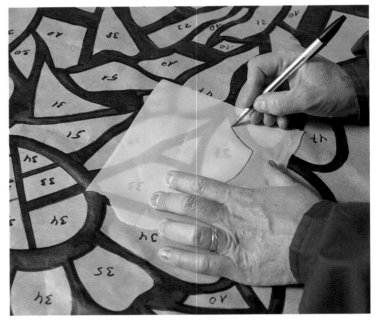

▲ **11.** The most appropriate dalles are selected for this particular job. They are usually about 12 inches (30 cm) long by 8 inches (20 cm) wide and 3/4 inch (2 cm) thick.

▲ **12.** The different glass pieces are traced onto vellum paper to make the templates.

◀ **13.** The template is attached to the surface of the glass with water. The glass is cut with a diamond disc machine.

▲ **14.** The dalles can also be cut with a cutting tool. The contour of the shape that is to be cut is first marked.

▲ **15.** The glass is placed on the cutting wedge and pieces are removed with a hard blow of the hammer.

◀ **16.** View of the glass after the previous step.

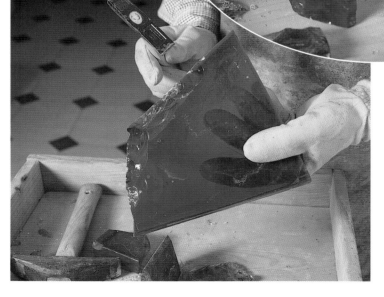

▲ **17.** One way to make the glass more interesting is to chip off pieces by striking it with the hammer.

▶ **18.** The cut dalles are set over the plastic, on their place in the drawing.

121

▲ **19.** The dalles are glued to the base with a few drops of fast-drying glue, to prevent them from moving when the cement is poured.

▲ **20.** The dalles must be put in place carefully to prevent them from touching the rods of the framework. The glue takes 30 minutes to set.

▼ **21.** All the glass pieces placed inside the framework.

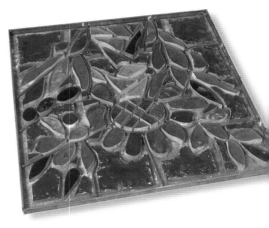

◄ **22.** General view of several stained glass panels moments before the cement is poured. It is possible to make large stained glass pieces with this method.

▲ **23.** Tools and materials that will be used to mix the cement. It should be mixed in the following proportions: 10 parts sand (100 g) to 3 parts gray cement (30 g). If white color cement is desired, 10 parts marble (100 g) should be used for 4 parts of white cement (40 g).

▲ **24**. The ingredients are mixed well to eliminate any of the lumps that may form.

▶ **26**. The ingredients are mixed thoroughly.

▲ **25**. Water is added.

▼ **27**. The lumps are broken up to prevent holes from forming in the cement. Rubber gloves are worn to protect the hands.

▶ **28**. A small container is used when filling the panel, to better control the amount of cement that is being poured.

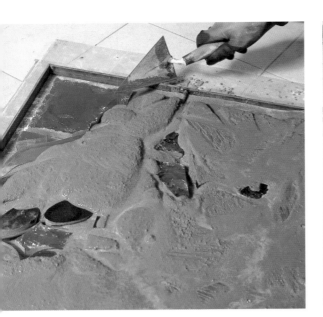

◄ **30.** Also, with the pointed end of the trowel, the cement is "poked" to eliminate the air that may form in the mixture.

▲ **29.** A trowel is used to tap on the structure to make it vibrate, forcing the cement to penetrate the spaces.

► **31.** The entire surface of the stained glass is covered with the cement, burying the dalles to make it more solid.

▲ **32.** The cement will take between 9 and 18 hours to dry, depending on the temperature. White Portland cement dries faster: 13 hours in cold temperature and 7 hours in hot. When the cement begins to dry, the top layer of it is removed.

► **33.** Straw is used to clean traces of cement that are still on the glass pieces.

◀ **34.** Hard-to-reach areas are cleaned with a brush with metal bristles. The cleaning is finished when the brush no longer "catches."

▶ **35.** Details of the stained glass. The two techniques used are visible: the dalles cut with a diamond cutter and the ones cut and chipped with a hammer (blue glass pieces).

▶ **36.** The completed panel. Note that the perimeter of the stained glass has a border of cement 1¹/₄ inch (3 cm) wide, which reinforces and holds all the dalles in place.

Stained Glass with Silicone

*T*o make a stained glass panel with silicone, the same procedure is followed as with any other type of stained glass. Only the support changes, which in this case is a sheet of glass, eliminating the lead came and the cement. In general, this sheet of glass is usually transparent, 1/4 or 1/3 inch (6 or 8 mm) thick and a panel made with it can be characterized as being tempered, laminated, textured with acid, and insulating.

In this project, double-panel insulated glass is used. The stained glass design is divided into 20 parts or pieces, it has an aluminum structure, and it is held in place with a wood frame. The glass pieces used in its construction can be of several types: cathedral, textured, blown antique, among others.

Because silicone is a viscous medium and therefore malleable, it adapts to the irregular surface of a given piece of glass. Unlike adhesives, it maintains elasticity, is stable under ultraviolet rays, is resistant to changes in temperature, sets in 3 hours, and cures in 48 hours. Pieces with large dimensions can be made without reinforcements. The only thing to keep in mind is the weight of the piece.

▲ **1.** Preliminary drawings and the final design done in watercolor at a scale of 1:12.

▲ **2.** The drawing to 1:12 scale is transferred to a full-scale drawing. The finished size of the stained glass is 8 by 23 feet (2.5 × 7 m).

◄ **3.** Once the full-size drawing is finished, a tracing is made, and a number is assigned to each glass piece.

▶ **4.** Tracing is done using carbon paper. A heavyweight paper is used for the templates, which later will act as a guide for the glass cutter.

◄ **5.** The templates are cut out with regular scissors, a cutter, or a utility knife.

◄▲ **6 and 7.** Once the colors for the glass have been selected, they are cut using the templates.

◄ **8.** Once the glass is cut, all the edges are smoothed with a belt polisher to prevent accidents while they are being handled.

► **9.** The backing glass is cleaned of any grime, dust, or oils, using a cloth dampened in alcohol.

▲ **10.** With a few strips of wood, stops are made to make it easier to hold the glass in place.

▶ **11.** When the glass is very thick, it is better not to put the full-size drawing underneath it, but to place it on the side with the glass pieces. Then silicone is spread over the surface of the glass.

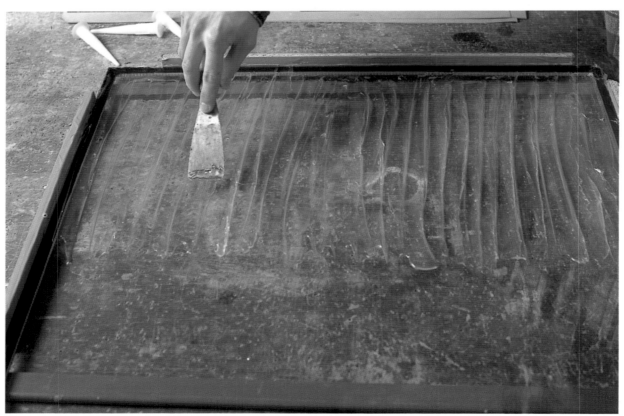

◀ **12.** The silicone is evenly spread over the surface with a spatula.

▲ **13.** The stained glass pieces are pressed and adjusted as they are placed over the silicone.

▶ **14.** If necessary, weights may be placed over the glass to cause the silicone to come out of the sides, which will prevent the formation of bubbles.

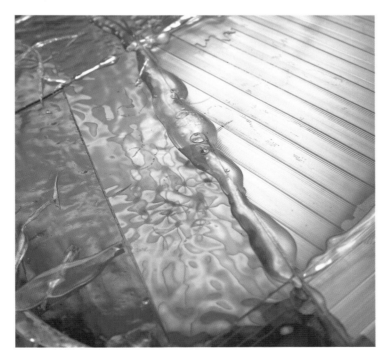

▲ **15.** Silicone coming out of the sides of the glass. This ensures that the edges will be sealed.

▶ **16.** The glass pieces are set in place along the sides by first leaning them on one edge and lowering them little by little, to prevent air bubbles.

▲ 17. It is better to wait at least 48 hours, depending on the temperature of the room, for the silicone to dry completely. Once it has dried, cleanup can begin.

▶ 18. Dry silicone cleans up very easily when it is cut with a spatula, a cutter, or a utility knife.

▼ 19. A special cleanser is used to soften the areas with stubborn silicone and to remove the traces that it leaves on the glass when it is removed.

▼ 20. If cleaning becomes difficult because of the texture of the glass, a brush with metal bristles can be used.

▲ ▼ **21. and 22.** View of the glass panel once it is completely clean.

▶ **23.** The completed stained glass panel, mounted on its aluminum structure and installed in the place for which it was designed—the parish church of Saint Joan de Vilatorrada, in the province of Barcelona, Spain.

Restoring
Stained Glass

The skills of the stained glass artist can also be applied to restoration projects. The restorer of stained glass must have not only a vast technical experience but also ample knowledge of the history of stained glass so the style of the period and the author of the work of art that is to be restored can be identified and interpreted. Keep in mind that in restoration there have been many tendencies or ways of interpreting the work. Basically three main schools of thought can be identified: the first one, proposed in the nineteenth century by the French architect Viollet-le-Duc, supports the stylistic unity of the work of art that is being restored, to such extent that it can result in a forgery or complete alteration of the entire piece. The second, also defended in the nineteenth century by intellectual artists and romantics, was led by Ruskin, who believed that the degradation and deterioration give esthetic and artistic value to the work of art, which must be maintained and respected. The third one, supported by Luca Beltrami, is the one that is most favored today, and it is based on the study of the documents, an in-depth analysis of the work of art that is to be restored and the respect for the portions that do not need restoring, and the artistic and esthetic criteria of its author.

Ultimately, the participation of the restorer must be limited to the consolidation of the area requiring restoration and the replacement of the damaged pieces, founded on the complete analysis of the work of art from a technical, historical, and artistic point of view. Also, we should keep in mind that restoration must always be reversible, that is, that it can be subject to revisions, and if necessary, to changes, if the latest studies and technological advances call for it. In the following pages we explain which steps are required in carrying out a restoration. Since no two restoration projects are exactly alike, a few general rules will be presented, which will be applied according to the needs of the work of art, although one must always keep in mind that the best restoration is good conservation.

Two examples of restoration projects will be presented, in the form of exercises: the replacement of a few glass pieces missing from a panel, and the restoration of a leaded stained glass window.

Before we begin the detailed description of the most important procedures in restoration, however, we list below the basic steps that the restorer must follow in his or her work.

To repair a stained glass work with a human figure whose broken glass pieces were previously restored with lead came:
1. Remove the lead came.
2. Glue all the broken glass pieces.
3. Protect the damaged area with clear plate glass.
4. Touch up the grisaille of the figure with Paraloid-type synthetic resin mixed with new grisaille paint.

To replace part of the grisaille:
1. Clean the affected area.
2. Protect it with clear glass.
3. Paint new grisaille over the corresponding area on the clear glass and fire the piece.

To fix the grisaille (experimental method):
1. Clean the damaged area.
2. Apply Paraloid-type synthetic resin mixed with acetone in a proportion of 3%.

▲ Stained glass window removed from its structure for restoration. Notice the broken lead came that frames the stained glass, the grime, and the broken and missing glass pieces.

▲ The stained glass piece after restoration. Some lead came pieces have been soldered over and others have been replaced with new pieces. Also, the glass has been glued into place to avoid distorting the design. And a red triangular piece, next to the figure of the rock on the left, has been replaced.

In the restoration or conservation of a stained glass piece, the three most common procedures are reparation, replacement, and cleaning. These three procedures will be demonstrated with practical examples taken from the restoration of stained glass windows from the thirteenth and fifteenth centuries.

▶ Detail of a stained glass piece depicting the image of Christ. This piece underwent a restoration previously, where lead came was used to hold the broken pieces in place. Notice that it is covered with dirt, and the grisaille is missing in some areas.

◀ The same stained glass piece after a new restoration. The lead came that was holding the broken pieces in the area of the face of Jesus has been removed and the pieces glued back together to avoid distorting the figure. Also, the piece has been thoroughly cleaned and the grisaille has been repaired.

▲ Putty should be used to repair a stained glass piece only in cases where there is no risk to the paint. Putty can be applied to the entire piece to repair the lead came or to make a minor repair, such as to cover a hole or to repair a specific piece of glass that moved because of a lack of putty.

Reparation

Repairing the Structure

Repairing a structure entails, in the first place, analyzing the support or frame that holds the stained glass and repairing it or replacing it if necessary.

The use of shims to fit the stained glass to its frame or to function as a fastener, peg, or wedge, makes the task of repairing it easier. The restorer may be able to make these wedges with the material that best suits the project (for example, stone, wood, or metal).

The condition of the bracing or rods should be checked and it should also be verified that the stained glass has no curvature as a result of the elements or due to an improper fit.

◀ Different types of wedges and pegs used to hold the stained glass in its structure. Black neoprene wedges. Pliers with cutting pincers, whose pointed ends are useful for cutting the wires from the rods.

Repairing the Lead Came

To repair lead came pieces, they must be looked over and catalogued by century. After an evaluation, the soldered joints are reinforced and the pieces of lead came that have suffered serious damage are replaced. Commonly, lead came pieces will break because of movement or the concave shape of the panel, which is the result of the pressure exerted by the wind. This type of breakage can be repaired easily by adding a drop of solder to reinforce the lead came. In the cases where the grisaille allows it, another way to repair the lead came is by reapplying putty to the stained glass piece.

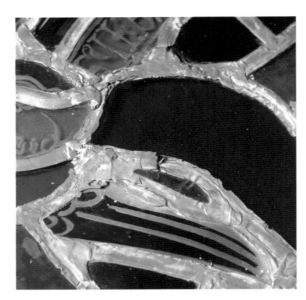

◀ 1. In the center of the picture, notice the broken lead came on a stained glass dating back to the thirteenth century. The lead came, dating to the eighteenth century, may be salvaged if the soldered joints are reinforced and the break is repaired with solder.

▼ 3. Before the lead came is soldered, the surface of the old came is scraped to remove the oxidation, and then flux is spread on the joint.

▶ 2. The sides of the lead came are lifted carefully, because the lead came used in the eighteenth century was very thin, and new small pieces of came are inserted between the old came and the glass. The procedure is repeated on the other side of the stained glass. Then, the lead came is flattened to form a single piece.

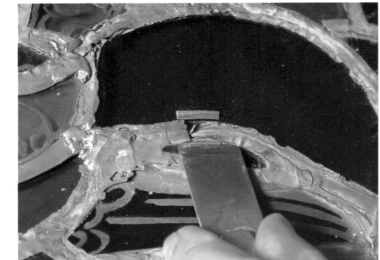

◀ 4. An electric soldering iron and a bar of 55 percent tin solder are used to join the broken section. The new pieces of came will prevent the solder from running through the spaces between the broken came.

▶ 5. The result of the soldering. As a general rule, a drop of solder will not adhere properly to an old piece of lead came and the soldered joint will not look perfect; however, the important thing is to repair the break. Notice also that a new piece of lead came has been applied around the face painted with grisaille.

Repairing the Glass

Repairing glass first requires the removal of the lead came that supports the broken pieces and that makes analysis and evaluation of them difficult. Next, the broken glass pieces must be glued back together, with resin or glue. To choose the most appropriate resin or glue, a test should be conducted on the pieces that need to be fixed. For added durability they can be reinforced with transparent glass.

Adhesive tape (transparent or opaque, made of plastic or paper) helps to hold the pieces in place until they are incorporated. When the lead came is broken, the pieces of glass should be held with tape so they will not come apart while being taken out and transferred to the studio. Attaching one piece of glass to another is a particularly delicate operation when the grisaille is in bad condition, because it was not fired properly, or because it came off due to the thickness of the layer.

The glues and adhesives used in the repair must be reversible, with the use of either acetone or heat. These can be found in any specialized store. Color may also be applied to the glues and adhesives, using the colors available in specialized stores.

Repairing the Grisaille

Grisaille can be repaired by applying synthetic resin mixed with 2.5 percent or 3 percent toluene or acetone. This resin, mixed with new grisaille, serves to recover specific areas or traces of the original grisaille. To protect the weakened grisaille, the particular piece may be covered with a transparent glass.

▲ 1. Picture of the stained glass before it is taken apart to begin the restoration process.

▼ 2. Applying synthetic resin with a syringe to repair the features that are missing in the figure.

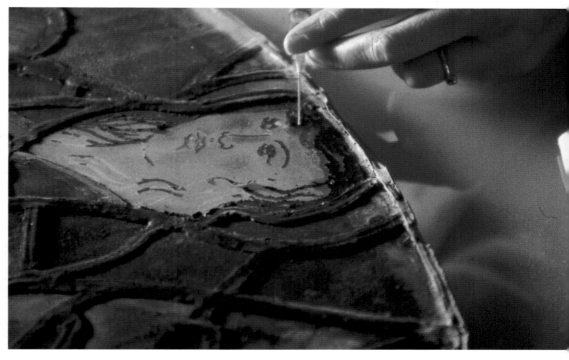

◄ Detail of a stained glass piece depicting a face in very poor condition. The grisaille has been repaired and the figure has been protected with transparent glass.

Replacing Components

Before any material is replaced, all elements should be evaluated and their authenticity checked. Substitution or replacement should only be done after careful study of the piece.

Replacing the Structure

Stainless steel is normally used to replace a structure. However, this is a task for a metal worker, who will make the structure following the measurements and the instructions that the restorer gives.

The reinforcement rods must be replaced when they are missing or are in very bad condition. To do this, pointed pliers should be used, which will break the supporting wires.

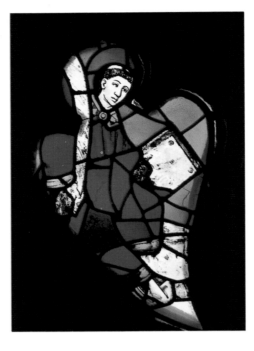

◄ This image is an example of a restoration where intervention has been minimal. The pieces of glass that were damaged or missing from the center of the piece had to be replaced with other neutral ones.

Replacing the Lead Came

The lead came should be replaced only if it is not sturdy enough because of breakage or because it is excessively soft.

The lead came is usually replaced with the same tools that stained glass artists normally use. The replacement can be total or partial. In a partial replacement, narrower lead came than the original may be used, to differentiate them. Total replacement of the lead came should be avoided, if possible, because an original piece of glass could break in the process of disassembling it.

At the same time the lead is being replaced, the soldered joints must also be checked and replaced if necessary.

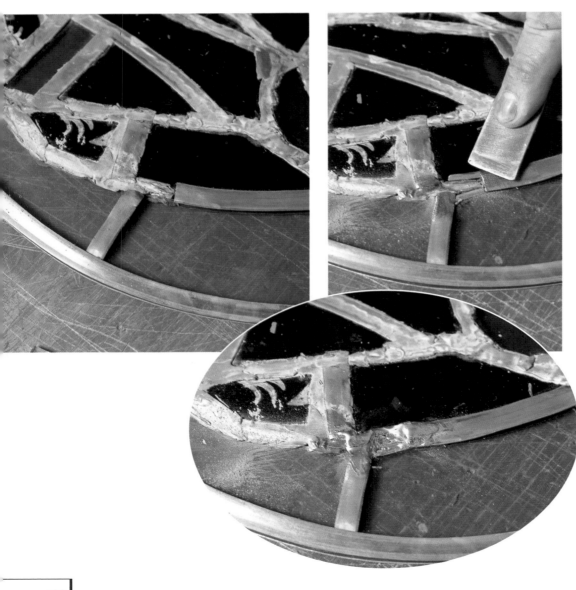

◄ 1. Replacing the lead came. The picture shows a partial replacement of lead came. The replacement was necessary because the old lead came could not be salvaged. The lead came should be replaced at the same time the glass is replaced. First, a clean cut is made in the damaged came and the new lead came is spliced to it. The new came can be the same width or narrower to differentiate it from the other.

◄ 2. Once the old came has been replaced, the stained glass is leaded following the traditional method. The came should be rounded so its faces can better hold the glass.

◄ 3. Flux is applied to all the joints and soldering is carried out with an electric soldering iron and 55 percent tin solder.

Replacing the Glass

When replacing glass that is beyond repair, either because it is broken or because it was improperly restored, it must be substituted with glass of the same characteristics and tones or with glass that is completely neutral, that is to say glass of the same chromatic value as the ones that surround the piece.

There are different ways to replace glass. In the old days, glass pieces of the same color or painted with grisaille from other restorations were used to replace glass that could not be repaired. In some instances, this procedure is not ideal because, for example, a part of a face may replace a piece of a robe, or an ornamental motif may replace a different one, or a section of yellow ribbon may replace blonde hair. However, it is difficult to distinguish these details in stained glass that is installed very high up, as it is usually the case in churches and cathedrals.

The most common practice nowadays is to use neutral glass to repair the loss of glass material. The photographs show this kind of glass replacement. Also, the new pieces have been attached with synthetic glue and not with lead came, which can distort the figures and produce false shapes.

◄ 1. Replacing glass pieces. A two-part synthetic glue will be used to attach the neutral glass that will replace the fragments of missing glass.

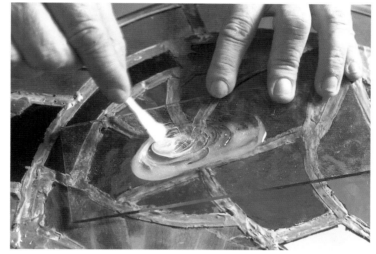

◄ 2. The synthetic glue is prepared, mixing the two parts thoroughly until a homogenous paste is obtained.

▲ 3. The appropriate neutral glass is selected, in this case red in color. It is then cut to the correct size and shape. A thin layer of glue is applied around the entire edge of the glass.

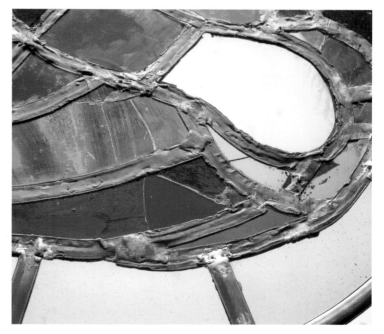

▲ 4. View of the red lobe restored in its tonality. Note in the foreground, the piece of red triangular-shaped glass that has been integrated into the original wing of the angel, also red, but painted with grisaille. Notice also the piece of neutral glass inserted in the area of the missing face and the small triangular piece of neutral glass incorporated into the original blue glass painted with grisaille to replace the lost glass.

Cleaning

A thorough cleaning of a stained glass panel accounts for 50 percent of a successful restoration. Returning the colors to their original state surprises even the most observant person.

A layer of grime and unfired paint are always found on the side that faces the interior of the building. The exterior face is usually cleaner because of the rain, but it is prone to mildew, which dulls the stained glass. Scraping solves this, which stops deterioration.

Always begin cleaning by first scratching one corner of the piece with a scalpel to determine the hardness of the layer that covers it. Before doing so, however, check the durability of the grisaille. Next, begin rubbing in circular motions with a brush; if good results are obtained, continue using these tools. Otherwise, use a cotton-tipped swab dipped in water to soften the layer of grime. If

this fails to remove it, use a neutral soap. This procedure is repeated on both sides of the stained glass. Because the inside of the glass is usually painted with grisaille, a magnifying glass should be used to distinguish between the grisaille and the layer of grime. The magnifying glass will also help in the cleaning of the mildew on the outside.

The piece that needs cleaning may also be dipped in a solution of 10 percent oxalic acid and distilled water. Because this product is toxic, precaution should be taken when using it.

Cleaning stained glass before it is restored requires specific tools, which are sometimes different from the ones that a stained glass restorer normally uses. For example, using blades of different sizes and shapes eases the task of removing grime and any unfired paint that may have been applied after the stained glass was made. A scalpel and a common utility knife for the less-delicate areas are

used to scrape through the layer of grime, and the brushes scrub, wipe, and pick up the grime accumulated on the surface.

Precaution should be taken when applying liquid products to remove the grime. It is a good idea to first test the product on a corner of the glass, at the edge of the glass panel. Keep in mind that cleaning with liquids does not afford the same kind of control as cleaning with a dry method; therefore the risk of damage is higher. It is best to simply use distilled water or tap water, mixed with a little bit of neutral soap. This can be applied with cotton swabs, the corner of a gauze pad, a sponge, or a cotton cloth for the most delicate areas. It is also advisable to use gloves for this procedure.

▲ **1.** A piece of stained glass affected by mildew. The calcified powder that is produced by scraping the layer of grime with a scalpel is the result of deterioration and weakening of the glass.

▶ **2.** The same piece of glass after a thorough cleaning. The calcified coating that covered the surface of the piece has been removed; however, the craters and cracks produced by the mildew could not be repaired, so the glass will always be somewhat opaque.

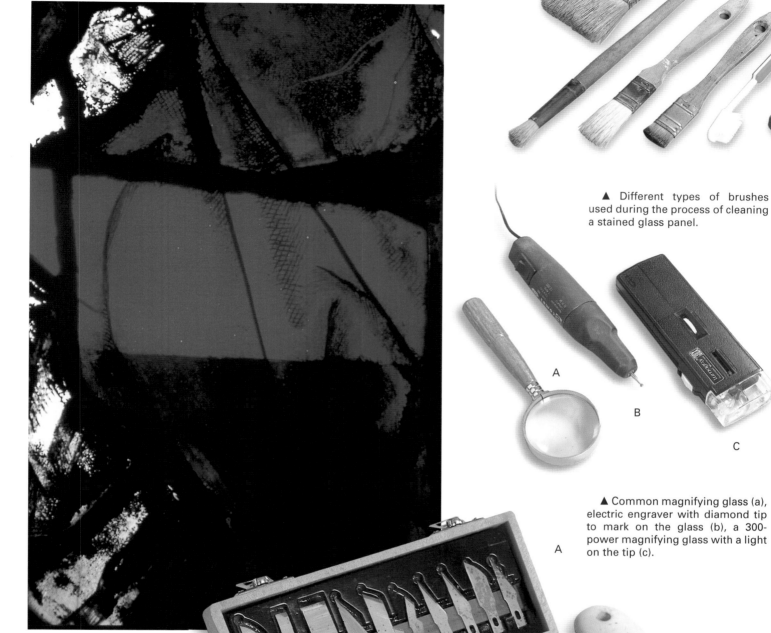

▲ Different types of brushes used during the process of cleaning a stained glass panel.

▲ Common magnifying glass (a), electric engraver with diamond tip to mark on the glass (b), a 300-power magnifying glass with a light on the tip (c).

▲ Detail of stained glass that has been carefully cleaned on the interior side.

▶ Tools used for cleaning: kit with various blades of different shapes to clean the glass and for hard-to-reach corners (a), scalpel (b), and common blade used for cleaning large surfaces (c).

Replacing Missing Glass

*M*ore than one approach can be used to restore stained glass. In this case, I have followed the steps that I considered most appropriate, based on my experience and training.

In the following pages, I will explain how to replace sections of some the faces and part of the clothing that are missing, for which there is no information other than the style used in the rest of the panel. I will also show how to attach some braces held with wire. Although I believe that if the reinforcements were soldered instead of secured with wires they would provide better support to the panel, I have chosen not to alter the piece any more than is needed.

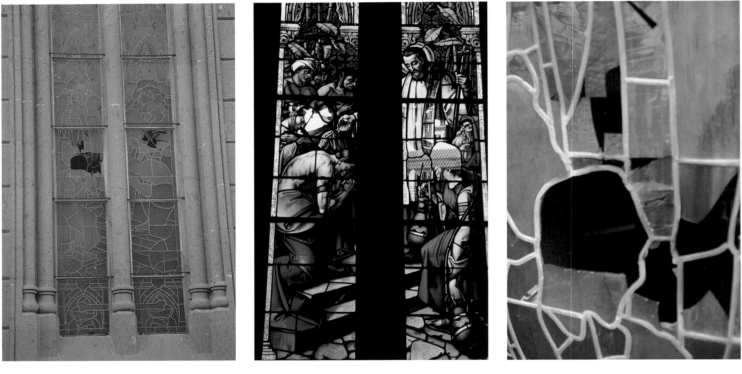

▲ Condition of the stained glass before restoration. The dimensions of each panel are 18½ inches (46 cm) wide by 27½ inches (69 cm) high.

▲ Partial view of the stained glass from the inside of the church of Arucas, in Gran Canaria, Spain.

▲ Detail of the broken pieces of the stained glass possibly caused by a hard blow.

► 1. Securing the damaged glass pieces with adhesive tape provides protection during transportation.

◄ 2. After securing the stained glass window, it is removed from the iron frame, carefully scraping away the putty that holds it in place.

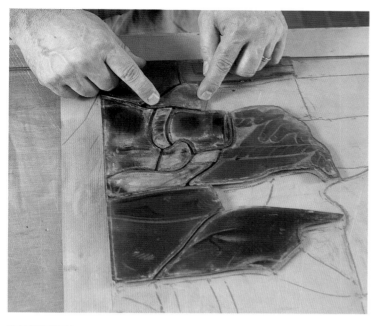

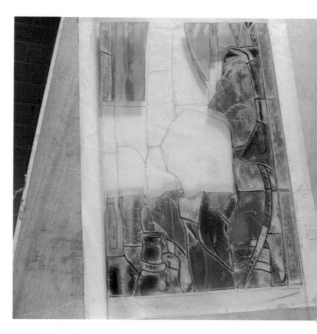

◄ **3.** The stained glass is taken apart in the studio after a copy of it is made.

► **4.** After the lead came is removed, the glass pieces are placed on a sheet of transparent glass with the drawing under it so it is easy to tell where each piece of glass belongs.

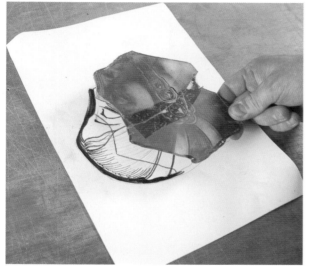

◄ **6.** This is repeated with all the pieces that have suffered any damage. This approach has been chosen so as not to interfere with the interpretation of the stained glass.

▲ **5.** The fragments of glass that belong to one of the damaged faces are put together, and the missing part is drawn to complete the silhouette.

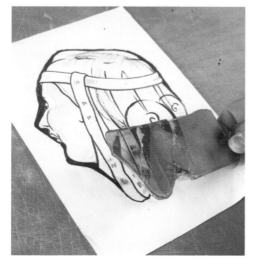

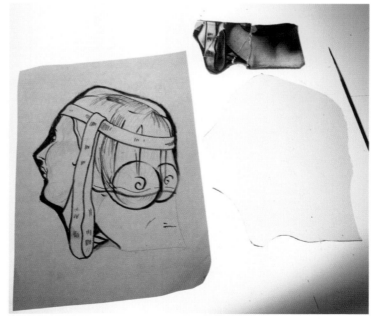

► **7.** In this face, only the bottom part is original. The rest has been reconstructed, based on the research that has been done.

► **8.** The base glass is cut to proceed with the design. As with the rest of the pieces, the original dictates the color.

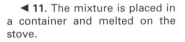

▲ 10. Beeswax is prepared and mixed with a little bit of rosin to attach the stained glass pieces to the sheet of transparent glass. A tool is devised from a piece of lead came that will be used to apply the mixture.

▲ 9. The lines that form the design are drawn with black grisaille.

◄ 11. The mixture is placed in a container and melted on the stove.

► 12. When the mixture acquires the consistency of a liquid, a drop is applied to each corner of the glass with the tool.

▼ 13. Following this procedure, the glass pieces are attached to the sheet of glass that serves as a base.

◄ 14. When the glass pieces are secured, the sheet may be lifted to paint it against the light, making the new pieces match those that surround them.

▲ **15.** Next, it is painted with brown grisaille, first applying a wash to the surface.

▲ **16.** A blending brush is used to smooth the coats of grisaille.

◄ **17.** When the grisaille is dry, shading and modeling is done with thin, dry brushes.

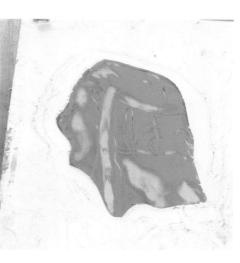

► **18.** When this is done, the glass pieces are placed on a steel sheet covered with dehydrated plaster powder and fired at 1,112°F (600°C).

► **19.** The piece immmediately after it is taken out of the kiln.

► **20.** Next, the piece is catalogued; the date of the restoration and the name of the person who did it are marked on the piece with a diamond point. This way, if another restoration is needed later, more information will be available.

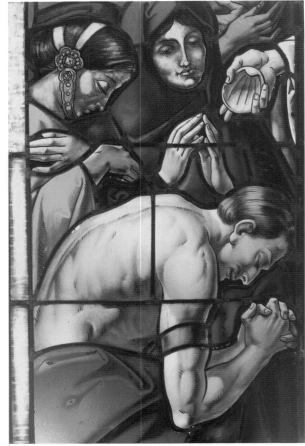

▲ **21.** The piece is returned to its place in the stained glass panel, and the result is checked. Then the pieces are leaded using the traditional method.

▲ **22.** The stained glass panel with lead came in place and ready for installation. Notice the glass that has been replaced by comparing this picture with the one in step 4.

▲ **23.** The restored panel where the two faces and the blue robe have been incorporated. Compare it with steps 5 and 6.

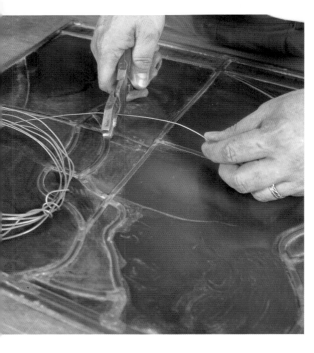

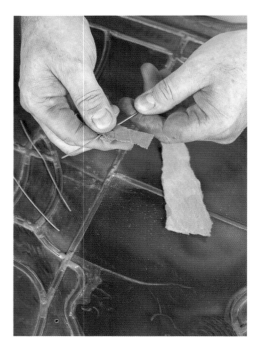

▲ **24.** Next, a few pieces of galvanized wire, which will be used to hold the support rods for the panel in place, are cut.

▲ **25.** All the oxidation of the solder is meticulously brushed off so the galvanized wires can later be soldered to the came.

▲ **26.** A small part of the galvanized coating of the wire is removed, using a sheet of emery paper, so the solder can adhere properly.

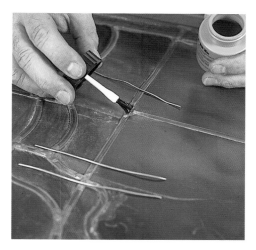

▲ 27. Flux should be applied so that a good joint can be made.

▲ 28. The galvanized wires have to be placed perpendicular to the reinforcement rod.

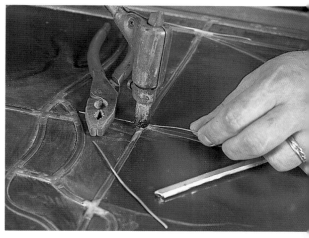

▲ 29. The wires are attached with solder. To do this, they are covered with a drop of tin solder, which will flow onto the came.

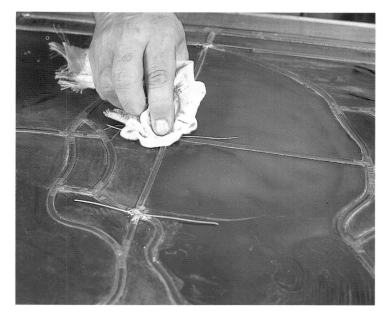

◄ 30. Next, the solder is cleaned.

► 31. The wire is twisted with pliers until the reinforcement rod is secured.

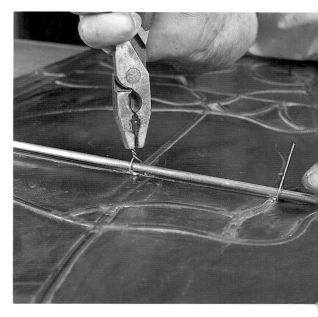

▼ 33. Once the wire has been twisted, it is folded over the reinforcement rod. There is enough left-over wire to repeat the operation in the other direction.

▼ 32. The wire should be long enough so the task can be carried out easily.

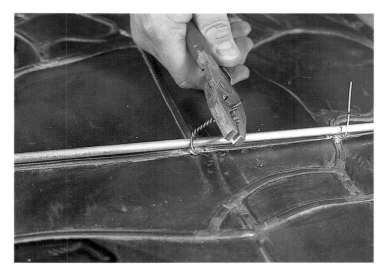

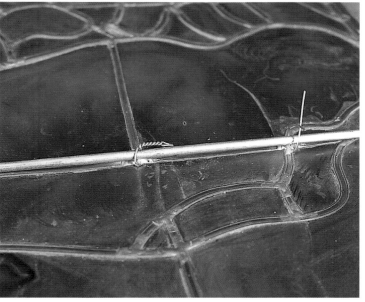

How to Restore Stained Glass with Lead Came

*F*or this restoration project, I have chosen an example that requires more steps. These are leaded stained glass panels made for various openings located in the highest part of the church of Our Lady of Pompeii, in Barcelona, Spain, dating back to the beginning of the twentieth century. The first step in a restoration project involves systematically studying the piece that needs to be restored. Before starting this project, all agents that have contributed to the damage over time must be analyzed, up to the present condition of the piece. Each restoration is unique, so one cannot be compared to another.

These openings located in the upper part of the building had a practical function, which was to vent the hot air that was generated and that accumulated in the vault. The iron frames have become deformed from constant opening and closing. This is the main reason why the stained glass pieces were constantly breaking.

Three previous restorations can be detected. One of them was a quick fix that became permanent. Once the stained glass was in the studio, it also became apparent that some glass pieces were painted but not fired, painted and textured with oil paints and held in place with lead came, with silicone, and so on.

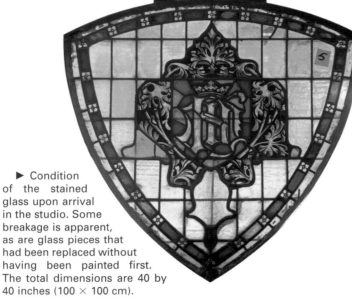

► Condition of the stained glass upon arrival in the studio. Some breakage is apparent, as are glass pieces that had been replaced without having been painted first. The total dimensions are 40 by 40 inches (100 × 100 cm).

▲ Detail of a previous restoration. A green piece of glass had been used to replace the broken one, which had been painted with grisaille.

◄ The reinforcements that protected the stained glass had been soldered to the structure. When the latter was moved, the reinforcements themselves caused the glass to break.

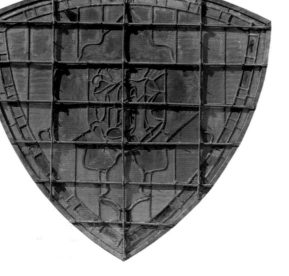

► **1.** Cutting pliers are used for cutting the copper wires so the stained glass can be removed from the structure. Notice the dirt caused by the soot, the smoke of the candles, and the passage of time. This is the dirtiest side, which was facing the inside of the church.

◄ 2. Detail of the task where the putty that holds the stained glass is removed. This operation must be done very carefully because there is a risk of breaking the glass. A spatula, a hammer, and pliers are the appropriate tools for this task.

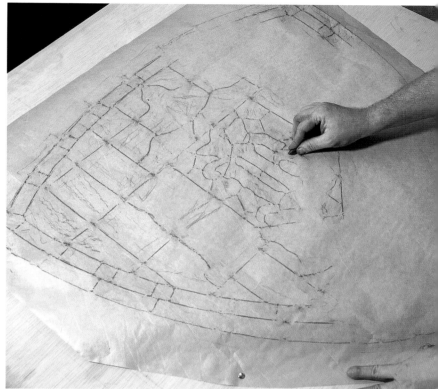

▲ 3. A tracing of the stained glass panel is made by rubbing graphite on paper. This step is done to study the design, in case it has been altered, and so the pieces can be placed on it after they are removed.

▲ 4. By comparing the traced design with the stained glass, a restorer can check if any piece was left out, and the drawing can be corrected if the stained glass had been modified by adding of lead came to hold broken glass pieces in place.

► 5. Taking the stained glass apart. The lead came must be cut with pliers or with a lead knife. This should be done very carefully, while removing the traces of dried putty from the edges of the glass pieces.

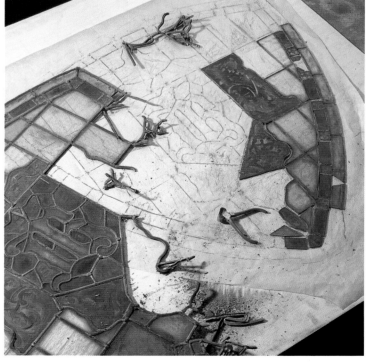

▲ **6.** Notice the face of the lead came, which covers a broken area, but does not reinforce it. It is a common practice when repairing stained glass to simply hide breaks. Also, on the upper part, there are two glass pieces of different qualities, which is the result of a previous restoration.

◄ **7.** The bottom part shows a painted glass piece, which is a copy of the original design. It was replaced with one painted with grisaille and fired at 1,112°F (600°C).

◄ **8.** View of the stained glass with the lead came removed. Nineteen pieces of glass were replaced in this panel by base glass and are now ready to be painted. In many windows, broken pieces are not detected until the lead came is removed.

▼ **9.** A broken piece is put together so it can be copied onto the one that will replace it. This procedure is applied to all the pieces seen in the previous photograph, especially to those that after being leaded would deform the design.

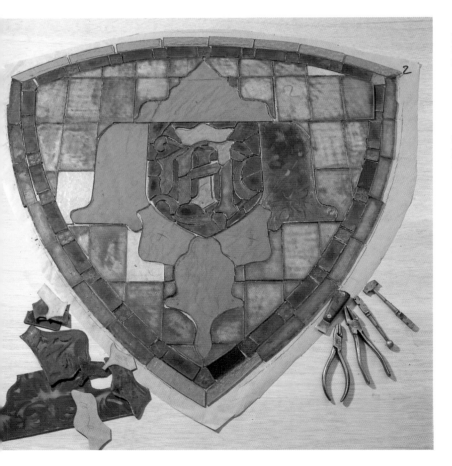

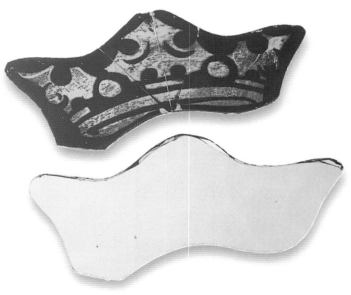

◀ **10.** The design being drawn with black grisaille. A fine brush must be used and hands must be rested on a bridge.

▼ **11.** When the design is finished, an inscription can be seen at one side of the piece. It is the restoration date. All of the replaced pieces should be marked, since they will provide information for a subsequent restoration.

◀ **12.** The first wash or *lavis* is applied with brown grisaille.

▼ **13.** The grisaille is spread and evened out with a badger, resulting in a brownish wash.

151

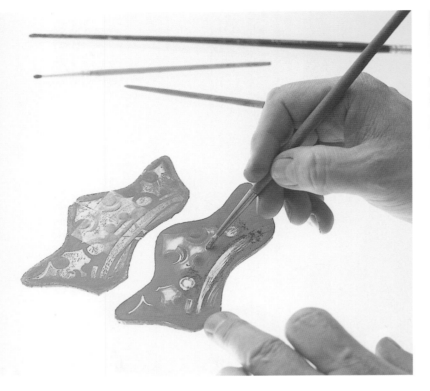

▲ **14.** When the grisaille has dried, the paint is modeled or the grisaille highlighted so that light can pass through.

▲ **15.** When the modeling is finished, the pieces are placed on a steel sheet with a layer of water-repellent plaster, and they are fired at 1,112°F (600°C).

◄ **16.** When the pieces come out of the kiln, lead came is applied, using the same width as the one used in the original, in this case, 1/4 inch (7 mm).

▲ **17.** The reinforcing rods are put back in place after the lead came and putty are applied, and the piece is cleaned. In this photograph flux is being applied.

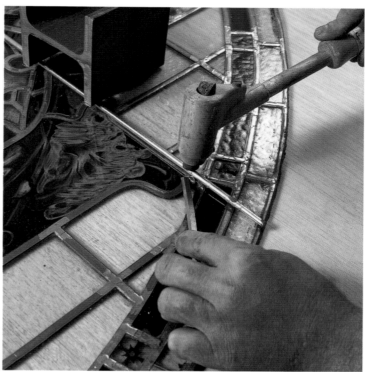

▲ **18.** Tin solder is melted between the galvanized steel bar and the lead came. The weight seen in the upper part of this illustration prevents the rod from moving during soldering.

▲ **19.** The iron rod must be hot for the solder to melt. One or two drops of solder are applied to the rod to hold it in place, and then the soldering is completed.

▶ **20.** With the stained glass sitting in the frame, wooden pegs are placed in the same holes where the previous pegs were located.

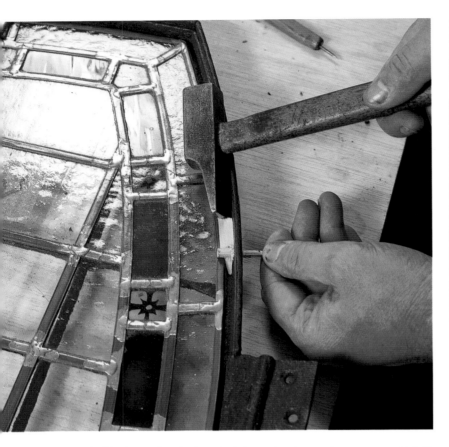

▲ **21.** A wedge is inserted in order to apply pressure and to immobilize the stained glass.

▲ **22.** Once the wedges and the pegs are in place, the excess pieces are cut off.

▼ **23.** The putty is kneaded until it acquires the proper consistency for use.

▼ **24.** Putty is applied around the edges of the restored stained glass piece.

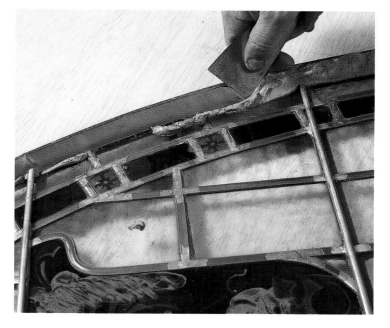

▲ **25.** The putty is pressed and the excess removed with a spatula. It takes 15 to 30 days for the putty to dry completely. In the meantime, the wedges and the pegs hold the stained glass in place.

▲ **26.** A detail of the lower section of the stained glass panel restored with lead came.

◄ **27.** The completed stained glass window. Compare it with the panel when it first arrived in the studio (pg. 148). The width at its widest point is 40 inches (100 cm), and the height at its highest point is also 40 inches (100 cm).

Glossary

a

Abrading. Technique for grinding the plaqué or matte glass in order to obtain different intensities of colors and tones.

Abrasion. Total or partial removal of a layer of flashed glass, by scraping, grinding, or using acid.

Acid etching. Process of removing a layer of flashed glass with hydrofluoric acid. The acid eats away the top layer of the surface and leaves another one of a lighter color uncovered. A matte finish is achieved with a mixture of hydrofluoric acid and soda crystals.

Annealing. Final cooling process of the surface of the glass, which tempers it.

Antique glass. Hand-made blown glass, which has an irregular texture, typical of medieval glass.

Apse. Semicircular or polygonal semivaulted area that protrudes from the back façade of a church.

b

Backing. Thin piece of transparent or colored glass used to reinforce fragments of old glass.

Badger blender. Wide, soft brush with hairs 3 to 4 inches (8–10 cm) long used to smooth out or to touch up a wash of paint.

Baroque. Artistic style developed in the seventeenth century and first part of the eighteenth, characterized by the use of curved lines and extravagant ornamentation.

Base colors. This refers to the original colors of the glass at its origin, when it is used as a base to which grisaille, enamel, acid, and so on is applied.

Beeswax. Material used for provisional assembly of stained glass pieces over a sheet of clear glass so that they can be painted or drawn on with grisaille. It is also used to make a container to hold acid.

Blown glass. Glass made in the form of cylinders or spun disks whose thickness ranges from $1/12$ to $1/4$ inch (2–7 mm). A single sheet can have different intensities of color.

Border. A band made with strips, geometric shapes, or plant forms, which could be discarded, to adjust the stained glass to the shape.

Bottle glass. Rarely used today, this type of glass is produced by blowing into a square mold, each side of which is cut into a sheet of glass.

Boudine. Also called bull's eye or knob, this protrusion appears in the center of a rondel, which was connected to the pontil that allowed the rotation of the piece.

Buttress. Support built onto the exterior of a wall to counteract the outward thrust of an interior arch, vault, or flying buttress.

c

Canopy. Glass framework in the shape of a niche within a window that surrounds a grouping of figures or a scene.

Cartoon. Full-size drawing of a composition or a figure that serves as a model for a work of art made with paints, mosaics, or stained glass.

Cathedral glass. Machine-made colored glass.

Cloisonné. Enameling in which the various colors are separated by *cloisons* or strips of metal, usually gold, soldered onto a metal base. This term is also applied to the stained glass made with metal strips and colored with small balls of colored glass.

Collage method. Pieces of colored glass bonded with epoxy to a clear sheet of glass.

Conservation. In stained glass, this refers to the process of checking, caring for, and replacing damaged pieces, putty, pins, or reinforcements of a stained glass piece so it does not deteriorate.

Corrosion. In stained glass, the destruction of the surface of the glass caused by humidity, grime, and pollution.

Crown glass. Piece of blown glass that is made by rotating the bubble until the shape of a disk with a central knob is created.

Cylinder glass. Most commonly used form of colored glass. It is made by cutting the edges of an elongated bubble, which is then split along its length to form a flattened sheet.

d

Design. Original model made in paper or three-dimensional mock-up, normally to a scale of 1:12, from which the full-size drawing is made.

Diapered. Covered with a geometric pattern made up of small squares.

e

Enamel. A vitrifiable substance that is applied to create color on glass and to reinforce it.

Enameled glass. Made by melting enamels on the surface of the glass.

Endomosaic. Combination of stained glass and mosaic.

Enlevé. The process of making highlights. The layer of grisaille, not fired, is scratched with wood or metal points to achieve a design.

Epoxy resin. Synthetic and colorless adhesive used instead of lead came to hold together pieces of colored glass, particularly *dalle de verre*.

f

Faces (of lead came). The outer portion of the **H** in lead came, which can be of various widths, that holds the glass in place.

Filet. Thin strip of glass or a grisaille profile.

Flashed glass. Two-layered glass made of a sheet of clear or colored glass with a thinner top layer.

Flying buttress. Arch or half-arch abutting against an outside wall and sitting on an outside support called a buttress. It is characteristic of the Gothic style.

Flux. Solvent, usually soda ash, used to help melt silica in glass manufacture. Borax is used to aid in the fusion of paint to glass.

Foil. Small opening in the form of an arch, typical of Gothic tracery, whose number characterizes its shape: trefoil (three), quatrefoil (four).

Fracture leading. Technique used to conserve a broken piece of glass, leading up pieces with a finer lead came.

Frame. Iron structure to which the web of wires is attached that protects the outside of the stained glass.

Fused glass. Pieces of colored glass that are heated until they bond to a sheet of glass.

g

Glasshouse pot. Container made of heat-resistant material that stands high temperatures and that is placed inside the central kiln where fusion of the components poured inside it takes place.

Glass paint. Enamel paint.

Gob. A portion of the molten glass that the glass blower takes out of the glasshouse pot.

Gothic. Artistic style developed in the Middle Ages whose main architectural characteristics are the use of pointed arches, flying buttresses, rib vaults, and tracery, and the reduction of the thickness of the walls, allowing for the openings of great windows covered with stained glass.

Grisaille. Black, brown, and so on vitrifiable paint made of iron or copper oxide and applied over the glass. It bonds to the glass when diluted with water or vinegar and gum arabic. It is fired at a temperature of about 1,112°F (600°C).

Grozing iron. Iron bar of rectangular shape with a series of notches of various widths, also rectangular in shape and with sharp edges, that is used to grind the glass and to remove its irregularities and sharp edges.

Grozing pliers. Tool used to nibble glass into shape once it is cut. It is usually made of soft iron.

h

Halation. A phenomenon that occurs when light-colored glass surrounded by stone or a dark frame produces blurred effects.

Heart (of lead came). The inner portion of the H in lead came. It is usually $1/16$ inch (2 mm) thick.

i

Insertion. Assembling one piece of glass or crown glass inside another piece of glass, normally of a different color, with lead came, copper foil, or silicone.

Isothermic protection. System of protective glass panels installed on the outside of the window openings.

j

Jesse Tree. Genealogical tree popular in many forms of medieval art, including stained glass, where Christ appears as a descendent of Jesse.

l

Lathekin. Small, sharpened piece of wood or bone used for opening and straightening leads.

Lead came web. Group of lead came pieces that hold together the glass pieces of a panel. Besides holding the stained glass pieces, the shape and widths of its lines contribute to the design of the stained glass.

Leading knife. Steel tool with a wooden handle that is used to cut the came during the process of leading up.

Leading up. Assembly of the glass pieces with lead came.

Lead shaping machine. Machine that has two steel wheels with teeth, spaced $1/16$ inch (2 mm) apart, with rollers through which the lead came is channeled to obtain the desired size.

Light. Opening between the mullions of a window.

m

Machine-rolled glass. Large-size glass that is made by pouring the molten glass onto a metal surface and passing a roller over it before cooling.

Mastic. See Putty.

Medallions. Stained glass made of panels of various shapes that are commonly arranged following in a narrative sequence.

Mold-blown glass. Glass blown into an opened top mold.

Muff. See Cylinder glass.

Muller. Tool made of granite or glass used to grind the grisaille or the enamel.

Mullion. Vertical stone shaft that divides windows or doors into lights.

o

Oculus. Round window, devoid of tracery.

Opalescent glass. Glass whose color, when fused, gives a milky, iridescent appearance.

Oxidation. The process of deterioration suffered by glass as a result of the oxidation of the reinforcement wires and the iron frame of the protective screen.

p

Painted glass. It refers to the colors that are added to the base colors through the use of grisaille, enamels, silver stain, sanguine, or Jean Cousin.

Panel. A window that is made of several pieces of glass.

Pattern. Full-size template for a piece of glass, made of construction paper or tracing paper.

Pattern shears. Double-bladed scissors that remove a strip that corresponds to the thickness of the heart of the lead came.

Pointed arch. Arch with two center points that cross each other. Characteristic of the Gothic style.

Pontil. Solid iron bar that is used to take the glass out of the glasshouse pot. It is 60 inches (1.50 m) long.

Pot glass, pot metal. Antique glass dyed in a single color.

Printed glass. Type of glass that is obtained through the action of acid or abrasive wheels.

Putty. Paste of high consistency that is used to encase the stained glass by inserting it inside the faces of the lead came. It is also used to attach the stained glass to the frame.

q

Quarry. Square or diamond-shaped pane of glass used particularly in stained glass.

r

Reamy glass. Irregular and streaky glass made from a mixture of glass of different degrees of hardness.

Reinforcement bar. Iron bar that is attached across the back of a stained glass panel.

Reinforcement rod. Pieces of rod used to reinforce the rigidity of glass panels. They are soldered to the lead came or attached to them with wire.

Rib. Structural or decorative salient edge that separates the sections of a vault. Used in Roman architecture.

Romanesque. Medieval artistic style whose main architectural characteristics are the round arch, the barrel vault, and thick walls and columns.

Rose window. Circular window with tracery in petal-like shapes.

S

Seedy glass. Antique glass with bubbles.

Silver stain. Silver compound, usually nitrate, that creates a yellowish tone when fused to glass.

Stippling. Technique used in painting that allows the creation of minute points of light over the grisaille on the surface of the glass.

Strap-work. Geometric shapes made of braided designs.

Streaky glass. Glass in which the color is not uniformly dispersed and therefore appears as streaks.

t

Temper. See Annealing.

Textured glass. Glass whose transparency has been reduced through the use of textures, patterns, or shapes.

Tiffany glass. Iridescent glass, patented by Tiffany in 1880, produced by exposing the hot glass to metallic fumes and oxides.

Trace painting. The act of drawing the lines or more pronounced details of a painting on glass. It is done with a brush with long hair, diluting the grisaille with vinegar.

Tracery. Architectural decorative feature made of geometric combinations that is displayed on door and window arches.

Trait. A more pronounced part of the outlining or contouring process done with grisaille over the glass.

Triforium. Arcaded gallery, sometimes covered with stained glass, found below the clerestory of a church.

V

Vault. Curved ceiling of a building. A tunnel vault is a vault with a semicircular section; a barrel vault is a vault formed by the intersection of two tunnel vaults at right angles; a ribbed vault is a vault that evolved from the barrel vault where the arches have been replaced by ribs that run diagonally and laterally and act as support.

W

Wash. Layer of very fine grisaille applied over the glass with the purpose of shading it and modeling it. Also called a *lavis*.

Bibliography and Acknowledgments

Brisac, Catherine. *Thousand Years of Stained Glass.* Edison: NJ BK Sales Inc., 1994.

Brown, Sarah. *Stained Glass: An Illustrated History.* New York: Random House Value, 1992.

Brown, Sarah and David O'Connor. *Glass Painters.* Medieval Craftsman Series. Toronto: University of Toronto Press, 1991.

Fruch, Erne and Florence Fruch. *Chicago Stained Glass.* Chicago: Loyola Press, 1983.

Heinz, Thomas A. *Frank Lloyd Wright's Stained Glass and Lightscreens.* Layton, UT: Gibbs Smith Publications, 2000.

Husband, Timothy. *The Luminous Image: Painted Glass Roundels in the Lowlands. 1480–1560.* New York: Metropolitan Museum of Art, 1995.

Isenberg, Anita and Seymour Isenberg. *How to Work in Stained Glass.* Iola, WI: Krause Publications, 1998.

Lyongrun, Arnold. *Masterpieces of Art Nouveau Stained Glass Design.* Mineola, NY: Dover, 1989.

Marks, Richard. *Stained Glass in England During the Middle Ages.* Toronto: University of Toronto Press, 1993.

Raguin, Virginia C., ed. *Conservation & Restoration of Stained Glass: An Owner's Guide.* Medford, MA: Census Stained, 1988.

Theophilus. *On Divers Arts: The Foremost Medieval Treatise on Painting, Glassmaking, & Metalwork.* John J. Hawthorne and Cyril S. Smith, translation from Latin. Mineola, NY: Dover, 1979.

Weiner, K. B. *The Stained Glass Guide.* New York: Watson-Guptill, 1994.

Williams, Jane W. *Bread, Wine & Money: The Windows of the Trades at Chartres Cathedral.* Chicago: University of Chicago Press, 1993.

I would like to thank all my professors of various disciplines for their invaluable teachings, through which I have finally come to realize that, in most cases, the solutions to the most difficult problems are found by following the simplest path.

I would also like to mention the invaluable collaboration of Tomás Constanzo, with whom I always consider it an honor to work. And I wish to express my gratitude to my editor, María Fernanda Canal, for her patience and understanding in the process of the production of this work.

I also want to add that the making of this book would not have been possible without the efforts, unconditional help and the encouragement of my wife, Neus, and my children, Lorena and David.

Pere Valldepérez